FRANK J. YARTZ, Ph.D., is an associate professor of philosophy at Loyola University of Chicago. At Loyola he teaches undergraduate and graduate courses in the history of philosophy, particularly in the areas of Plato, Aristotle, and Thomas Aquinas. He has published articles on ethics and Ancient Greek philosophy. His works appear in *Medieval Studies, Southwestern Journal of Philosophy,* and *Modern Schoolman.*

DAVID J. HASSEL, S.J., Ph.D., is an associate professor of philosophy at Loyola University of Chicago where he teaches courses in the Philosophy of Evolution, Metaphysics of Culture, Being and God, Philosophy of Man, Philosophy of Religion, Secularization Theory, and the Philosophy of St. Augustine. He has published a chapter in *Working Papers on Problems in American Life,* book reviews in the *Modern Schoolman* and *Theological Studies,* an article in *Proceedings of the Jesuit Philosophical Association.* He is presently completing two books.

ALLAN L. LARSON, Ph.D., is a professor of political science at Loyola University of Chicago, teaching both undergraduate and graduate courses in comparative political systems. His articles and essays on political and social science subjects have appeared in *Educational Forum, Social Studies, Social Education,* the *Midwest Quarterly,* and the *Delphian Quarterly.* He is currently writing a book on comparative political analysis.

PROGRESS
AND THE
CRISIS OF MAN

PROGRESS
AND THE
CRISIS OF MAN

Frank J. Yartz, Ph.D.
David J. Hassel, S.J., Ph.D.
Allan L. Larson, Ph.D.

Foreword by
Robert J. Roth, S.J., Ph.D.

Nelson-Hall nh Chicago

LIBRARY OF CONGRESS CATALOGING IN PUBLICATION DATA

Yartz, Frank J
    Progress and the crisis of man.

    Includes index.
      1. Civilization, Modern—1950-   2. Progress.
I. Hassel, David J., joint author.   II. Larson,
Allan L., joint author.   III. Title.
CB428.Y36   909.82   75-44451
ISBN 0-88229-165-3

Manufactured in the United States of America

Contents

Dedicated
to the memory of
GEORGE PETER KLUBERTANZ, S.J.
Author, Educator, Priest, Friend

Foreword

One of the criticisms most frequently voiced against the academic community by students on the graduate and undergraduate level is the isolation of disciplines into separate departments. One has ample opportunity, it is claimed, to study science, history, literature, philosophy, or whatever. But where is it possible for the student to relate these disciplines into a coherent picture so that he may assess the development of leading ideas that have shaped the present and make projections that will direct our future?

It is refreshing, then, to come upon a book that brings together two philosophers who are aware of the impact of science and a political scientist who knows his philosophy. Addressing themselves to the problem of progress, they have attempted to mark out some guidelines for evaluating its meaning and to suggest possible directions for the future. Aside from any other value the volume may have, it does provide much-needed relief from over-specialization and serves as a model of how experts from different fields can sit down and talk with one another on a common problem.

Professor Allan Larson indicts the scientist for being too preoccupied with scientific advance and not enough with its implications for human life. Some will say that the criticism is a bit unfair. After all, the scientist does have his own specialized problems and methodology. He proceeds on the assumption that every problem is an hypothesis which is always subject to challenge in the light of new empirical evidence. Without this assumption, science would stagnate and die. Moreover, not all scientists are unaware of or indifferent to the moral issues that arise regarding the uses made of scientific discoveries.

Yet more than one observer of the current scene has asked whether science and technology have gotten ahead of evaluation and have become concerned more with the quantitative than with the qualitative aspects of human experience. One immediately thinks of Alfred North Whitehead's *Science and the Modern World* of some thirty-five years ago in which a mathematician launched his philosophical career with such a critique of modern science. Professor Larson seems to feel that Whitehead's voice has not been sufficiently heard and that his thesis needs restating in view of the advances made in science since Whitehead's day, especially in the life sciences.

All this touches in a very crucial way upon the issue of progress and its meaning. Thus Professor Larson asks some pressing questions: *Ought* we to do all that we *can* do? Are we to control or back into the future? Should not scientific work, like every other kind of human endeavor, be subject to guidelines in the form of critical evaluation and moral judgment?

This in turn raises the question of how we are to define man. There are those who would view man solely in terms of his ability to carry out what he plans and designs. This would limit the meaning of the human to technological man. Other meanings, of course, easily come to mind. To cite but a few, one could consider man in terms of bone structure (evolutionary man), overt behavior such as tool-making (anthropological man), drives and needs (psychological man), unconscious motivations (psychoanalytic man), human relationships (social man), political structures (political man), or economic factors (economic man). If modern thought has taught us anything, it is that we can no longer view man from one perspective. A full picture can be delineated only by drawing on many disciplines. All of them make their unique contribution and must be considered. To omit any one is to lose sight of important dimensions.

Professor David Hassel has chosen to underscore the social dimension. He shows that largely under the impact of science man has become highly specialized in his activities, whether in the technical field of science or in everyday tasks. At the same time, by necessity man must integrate his activities with those of others if his field of specialization is to be exercised efficiently and improved. Social relations, then, are in a sense a necessary condition for progress in these areas.

But for these activities to be experienced as worthwhile, man must become aware of the needs of other individuals and groups of individuals, and he must consciously direct his energies toward the good of others. By such cooperation, individuals in community on ever-widening levels are enriched and fulfilled.

In spelling out the value of social awareness, Professor Hassel gives a hint as to what genuine progress means. No matter what else it may entail, progress must include the union of minds and wills engaged in activities which, while truly carried out by individuals, are at the same time exercised in cooperation with others and are directed toward goals that are shared in common. A purely atomic model is no more valid in social relationships than it is in science.

In developing his position, Professor Hassel has also underscored man's relationship to and responsibility for the material universe. He is opposed to a view of man that would overemphasize an otherworldly destiny and derogate the importance of this world for human development. However, he does not exclude mystery and myth, and in fact he criticizes any view of man that would omit them.

Professor Francis Yartz develops more explicitly some of the themes already discussed. For him, the real dilemma of progress is the fact that, in spite of undoubted scientific advances, there are numerous examples of disharmony among men. This makes one doubt whether civilization has really made significant progress. Professor Yartz then argues his own position that social relations are a criterion for progress, and he criticizes other thinkers who would oppose this view.

Any theory of social relationships must face up to the question of personal freedom and creativity. This really means that a viable social theory must develop some kind of harmony between the individual and the community, and a social philosopher will tend to be placed in this or that category depending on how he balances the two or where he places the emphasis. Professor Yartz, aware of this problem, develops his own position.

Any further elaboration of this book might distort its message and deprive the reader of the opportunity to make his own discoveries. I shall conclude, therefore, by making some observations.

The real value of the book is its daring attempt to assess progress in our present age. Not an easy subject to discuss, it is one that must be faced squarely and honestly. This the authors have done. In the process they have put their finger on some crucial issues: the need of moral commitment in a scientific age, the importance of social relationships, the delicate balance between individual and community, and the growing emphasis upon freedom and creativity within these contexts.

Whether the contributors to this volume intended it or not, their philosophical orientation moves in the mainstream of the so-called "golden age of American philosophy." I have already mentioned Whitehead, who was deeply concerned with the growth and progress of civilization, the role of science, with beauty, value, and the direction that the universe was taking. Charles Sanders Peirce approached these questions from an evolutionary stance, and hence evolutionary love stood at the apex of his thought. William James's keen sense of man's existential situation directed him to an intense interest in the quality of human experience. No American philosopher was more preoccupied than John Dewey with questions of value, science, social and political theory, and the kind of fulfillment that could be reached through human endeavor. All of these believed that the meaning of man and the meaning of progress could be understood only in terms of man's relationship with the material universe and especially with the world of people and communities.

One important task, however, remains to be done by the above-mentioned classical American philosophers and by the writers of this volume. It is to state clearly and precisely the criteria by which genuine progress is to be judged. This is the kind of task that one bravely assigns to others while shrinking from it oneself, and I would plead guilty to the charge of using this ploy. Surely our three authors have given suggestions as to what these criteria would be. By way of negation, one would not judge progress exclusively in terms of scientific advance. On the positive side, progress would include social harmony that comes from the sharing of common goals and of the means to attain these goals. But how is one to judge which goals are to be cherished and pursued and which to be eliminated? Human fulfillment, often proposed as the criterion for these goals, has been suggested more than once in the course of this volume. But again the same question returns: How are we to judge fulfillment?

Moreover, I am not sure whether the authors are operating within a purely naturalistic, "this-worldly" framework. It is stated here and there that criteria for progress need not, indeed must not, exclude a transcendent source and goal of human endeavor. But the point is not argued. I would like to see a more explicit position taken on this issue.

Beyond that, one would be carping. No easier statement can be made about a book than that it is in the long run inadequate. Any book on any subject usually is. But then we are mostly addressing ourselves to what a book does not say. I enjoyed what this book does say, and I recommend it to anyone who is seriously interested in assessing progress in our own times.

Robert J. Roth, S.J., Ph.D.,
Dean, Fordham University
Bronx, New York

Preface

One theory of social progress runs through and holds together the various chapters of this volume. It is that social progress is innovative social change anchored by human value. Deeply imbedded in the notion of human value is the fact that man is a social being—that is, man must enter into social relations with others to be man. Through social relations that benefit the individual as well as society, men of different viewpoints and unique personalities can nevertheless unite to form society. True social relations involve a unification of various ranks that naturally form in society—ranks established by education, wealth, ethnic background, and the like.

Despite the fact that this book advocates *one* theory of progress, *three* crises of social progress become apparent. The first crisis is that of technological progress.

Technological progress frequently disrupts the established living pattern and, as a result, society must learn to readjust to a new manner of thinking and living. Many times the disruption causes problems of so grave a nature that one is forced to ask: Is technological progress actually progress in an important sense of the word? Technological progress is really progressive only if, in its effort at benefiting man, it also seeks to control social change in the light of human value.

The second crisis which this volume probes is that of secularization versus secularism. As one proceeds to relate to others through his lifework, he carries along in this social relation his own values which influence those around him. For some this value orientation is God-centered; for others it is not at all. Secularism results from the spreading of the godless spirit in social relations. Secularization in itself is open to theistic awareness.

The theory advanced in Chapter II ultimately implies that the order of the sacred and the order of the secular do merge. The sacred and the secular cannot be considered only as ranks or orders, but must be dynamically related to each other. This relation unifies both the individual elements making up one's personality and also the multiple elements going into the development of society. The concept of a Christian education, for example, ought to include the best possible secular education; otherwise, it fails as Christian education.

The third crisis is the disagreement itself among many philosophers on the meaning of progress. For some philosophers a theory of social progress results in playing down the importance of the individual man. Other theories take into account man's individuality, but consider him as an atomic unrelated unit; thereby, these theories are hard pressed to explain the fact that man as individual enters into social relations. A workable philosophy of progress must be able to show that the progress of society results from the progress of individuals. Thus, in the final analysis, a theory of progress is only as good as the philosophy of man that animates it.

Finally, may I note that this book springs forth from the true social relation that it so heartily advocates. We are all indebted to our teachers of the past, students of the past and of the present, as well as many other colleagues. Special thanks are due to Robert J. Roth, S.J., Dean of the College of Arts and Sciences of Fordham University for his foreword, Dorothy J. Anderson of Nelson-Hall, and two chairmen for their encouragement, Frank J. Catania, Chairman of the Philosophy Department at Loyola of Chicago, and Thomas J. Bennett, Chairman of the Political Science Department at Loyola of Chicago. Conversations with John A. Hardon, S.J., of the Jesuit School of Theology and Lothar L. Nurnberger, S.J., of Loyola of Chicago have helped to improve the manuscript. In various ways the following have all helped in putting this book in its final form: M. Vogel, S.J., T. F. Hecht, S.J., R. J. Harvanek, S.J., C. R. Aita, Jr., M. Larson, M. E. Hayes, Michael O'Connor, S.J., and G. A. Yartz. I also wish to express thanks to the students in Dr. Larson's seminar, "The Idea of Progress Re-examined" which was held in spring, 1974: C. Craig, S. Crumrine, I. Goldstein, M. Mullin, E. Richards, J. Stadnik, and T. Stanfa.

Frank J. Yartz

chapter I

Allan L. Larson, Ph.D.

Progress and Crisis in Technological Civilization

THE AMBIGUITY OF THE IDEA OF PROGRESS

For the greater part of human history, the idea of social progress was not commonly held. Only with the breakdown of the feudal order and the emergence of a new society in Western Europe did the idea become established that human nature is subject to continuous improvement and that society as a whole is inevitably moving toward a better order of life.[1] It is difficult to appreciate how radical and subversive this idea must have seemed to most people of that time. To assert that man could change society to suit his needs and conveniences was to reject a vast collection of legends and laws.[2] The belief in progress was destined to inspire many of the great political and intellectual movements of modern Western civilization. It became a pervasive theme in the evolution of modern Western thought.[3]

Whether there is such a thing as "progress" in history depends, of course, on what we mean by the term. The fact of material progress became increasingly evident as

1

the nineteenth century unfolded its technological revolution. Progress consisted largely of the faith that technological changes would probably continue indefinitely to enrich human society by advancing prosperity and generally making people happier.[4] But the concept of progress is so elusive that attempts to define it are few. Even among the definitions that we do find, there is only limited agreement as to its precise nature. As soon as we begin to discuss the criteria for evaluating the progress of a society, we are launched into a world of ambiguity and complexity. In the words of Carl Becker, "The modern idea of progress belongs in the category of answers to necessary but insoluble questions. Like the myths of primitive peoples, it springs from the nature of man as a conscious creature, who finds existence intolerable unless he can enlarge his experience by relating it to something more enduring than himself."[5]

Precisely because it is so problematic, "Have we progressed?" is one of the most fascinating questions with which we can tantalize our minds. Different people look at the same social changes: to some they spell progress and to others regress. Whenever we speak of progress without a qualifying adjective such as "political" or "economic," we are invoking ultimate standards of value. Evaluations of progress thus depend upon the standard of value chosen for measuring it and upon the time perspective in which it is measured. These judgments are based on standards of value appreciable by the mind of civilized human beings. The assessment of change depends in most instances on what people in a given society consider desirable and undesirable. Every achievement has its costs; people of good will often differ as to whether the costs outweigh the values gained. To arrive at such social balance sheets is a difficult process, yet such an accounting is involved in every attribution of progress.

Etymologically speaking, the word "progress" means simply moving forward in a certain direction on a certain road (even if it happens to be a dangerous road). But the common denominator of the numerous definitions of social progress is the identification of progress with "change for the better." The idea of progress is thus bound up with the notion that time is redeeming. Progress is portrayed as constantly meeting problems and solving them successfully. The term plainly has reference to the future; it involves planning in order to promote the desired goals. We strive for specific objectives and imagine that each objective attained is a recognizable step toward "progress." The result of such thinking is that we are baffled when, having attained an objective, we encounter not the "progress" expected but a new set of problems stemming from the very advance itself. What constitutes an advance in one period may turn out to be a maladaptation or a regression in another era.

This Januslike quality in the evaluation of progress is why we cannot identify social progress with social evolution. That society has evolved is a demonstrable certainty; whether society has progressed is shrouded in ambiguity. The notion that each succeeding society or each succeeding age is somehow better than the preceding one is almost a dogma, to Americans in particular. But in all the great movements of political, economic, and social change there is loss as well as gain (whatever standards we adopt for our evaluations). In whatever we define as "progress," there is certainly not an equal advance of all the items in our catalog of goals. It is this complexity, perhaps, which has often led social analysts to suggest a single criterion by which the history of their society is to be judged; hence, the arguments of Hegel, Marx, Darwin, Freud, or Toynbee. Fundamental to any evaluation of progress is a set of criteria by which it can be measured. The problem is complicated by the fact that both qualitative and quantitative criteria are involved in such evaluations. If there has been a fundamental flaw in the development of Western civilization, it has been to identify the concept of progress with the belief that growth for growth's sake is a sure formula for the improvement of human life. This faith has been dominant since the beginning of the eighteenth century and is still widespread today.[6] Obviously, the whole ethos of the industrial world and its development have been based on growth. Politics, economics, and business strategy accept expansion as the right and proper object of "progress." However, by definition, no rate of growth can go on forever; every growth rate we know about will top out. Our generation is the first to realize that man will have to curtail growth; conceptions of progress must now come to terms with the situation of a planet of limited resources and of a delicately balanced environment which must be kept in equilibrium. Preserving the quality of life may soon be considered more important than promoting economic growth in the future balance sheets of progress.

Future conceptions of progress will likely be viewed in terms of transformations more than in terms of sheer quantitative growth. Present-day conceptions of politics, energy, information, man, woman, animal, planet, old age, death, knowledge, and time will be cast in new paradigms. The life of the future remains outside the scope of conventional wisdom. Solutions will not be found without new definitions of progress, based on better knowledge of nature and on a willingness to change our ways of life accordingly.

THE ROLE OF TECHNOLOGY IN CIVILIZATION

We can see the ambiguity of the idea of progress in thinking about the role of technology in modern society. The rapid changes of our society are obviously related to and dependent upon the development of new techniques, new inventions, new modes of production, new standards of living. The swift transitions of our technological civilization have been followed by far-reaching social changes, many of which appear to be necessary accommodations to the world of the machine. Much contemporary social criticism seeks to depict technology as anathema to a humane and just society. Defenders of technology reply that it is a set of neutral means; whether it is used to good or evil purposes is not determined by the technology itself. Both of these viewpoints are as valid as half-truths usually are. While some technological developments do promote an impersonal, efficiency-minded, mass-production society, it is equally apparent that other technologies are essential for a more humane and liberated society.[7]

Technology is older than science. All the records of early man indicate clearly that he created artifacts and evidently used them before he attempted any systematic account of the meaning of his activities. We should remind ourselves that early technology included the discovery and taming of fire for the production of warmth and the cooking of food, the sowing of seed and the cultivation of crops, the domestication of animals, the building of shelters for the living and tombs for the dead, and the progress from the age of stone to the age of metal.[8] From time immemorial, a large part of technology has been directly concerned with the creation of ingenious ways to make life richer and more comfortable for *homo sapiens*. Technology has been the mainspring of the changes responsible for evolutionary progress. Certain inventions and discoveries have been crucial to human evolution but it is important to realize that technological development is realized more by the incremental advancement of many small inventions than by the sudden discovery of revolutionary phenomena. Man's conquest of the natural world has been based upon his accumulated technological knowledge. This technology is always related to the environment. The Industrial Revolution destroyed the domestic system of production, brought women out of the home and into the world of commerce, differentiated their tasks and distinguished their earnings. This was a new environment and the new social life of women was the response. The rapid spread of modern technology offers a myriad of similar illustrations.[9] Attitudes, beliefs, traditions, and customs which were thought to be of the very essence of human nature have been significantly affected by the pressures generated by the advance of science and technology.

Technological growth has had an exponential quality; that is, the rate at which growth takes place increases with each successive increment of advancement. As technology becomes more elaborate, more specialization becomes necessary and people have less time to develop their total capacities. Technological civilization requires a continuous increase in the skill levels of its work force; these occupational specialties are combined in increasingly complex and "rational" ways to constitute the web of the technological society. The economic fabric of Western technology is far more elaborate, specialized, extended, improved, and refined than any other. Much of the improvement and elaboration of techniques is a consequence of the secularism in society. Secularism involves a transfer of primary concern from the spiritual to the material, from God to man. It includes a whole complex of ideas and philosophies that have to do with the world as it is and the empirical approach to history and society.[10]

The last century has witnessed a radical transformation in the entire human environment, largely as a result of the impact of the physical sciences upon technology. Technological advancement has opened up such new realms as nuclear energy, computer intelligence, the exploration of space, and genetic control. Because technological changes have accelerated so greatly during the past quarter century, scientists and philosophers alike have begun to question many of the fundamental assumptions underlying the uses of technology. Consider, for example, the Apollo missions to the moon. Only an incredibly torpid individual could fail to be moved by the brilliant precision that marked every step of the lunar landings. But what do the moon landings, impressive as they are in terms of awesome technology, mean for man on earth? Will they be recorded, ultimately, as the beginning of a great new era or only as an expensive vacation from earthly reality? Lewis Mumford has bluntly asserted:

> Although many now credulously believe that
> space travel will open up marvelous new
> possibilities, there are strong historic grounds for
> believing, rather, that this marks the fatal terminus
> of a process that has from the Pyramid Age on
> curbed human development. Any square mile of
> inhabited earth has more significance for man's

future than all the planets of the solar system. It is not the outermost reaches of space, but the innermost recesses of the human soul that now demand our most intense exploration and cultivation. The prime task of our age is not to conquer space but to overcome the institutionalized irrationalities that have sacrificed the values of life to the expansion of power, in all its demoralizing and dehumanizing forms.[11]

It would, of course, be absurd to "protest against science" and its most appropriate product, the machine. The natural sciences are simply extensions of our legitimate interest in the technical management of natural things to produce the results we desire. However, thoughtful men may question the sense of priorities that spurred us to spend thirty billion dollars exploring outer space while Planet Earth was confronted with social and economic paroxysms of an intensity greater than any we have so far known. Was it, indeed, only coincidental that the moon landings came in the midst of cutbacks in education, the bankruptcy of hospital services, the closing of libraries, and the mounting defilement of the natural and urban environment? Defenders of the prolonged exploration of outer space usually point out that the space budget never came to even one per cent of the gross national product of the United States. But the haunting question still remains: Could the thirty billion dollars have been disbursed for more significant human objectives? Or, considering the validity of the moon landings, why are we moving so slowly in our efforts to eradicate poverty, crime, and ignorance on this planet? One can be dazzled by astronauts striding on the moon and still yield to a sense of irony when looking at the unresolved physical and sociological diseases that afflict the masses of our fellow human beings on earth.

Now that the application of science to technology has so greatly increased mankind's aggregate skill and wealth, what are the correct priorities for the use of our resources? Lewis Mumford can hardly be dismissed as antiscience for asking whether the huge expenditures on space travel are justified while the great majority of the human race lives in poverty. It surely can be argued that the exploration of outer space, while in no way morally offensive in itself, should have been assigned a lower priority until the poor majority of the human race on the face of this planet was raised to the level of the rich minority. Then we could resume the space program with a good conscience and with a better moral position to indulge in this new adventure.

The social function of technology is to control and put to service in man's interests the rich variety of physical and biological phenomena. We cannot and should not turn off the switch of technological progress; a deliberate attempt to turn back the clock would condemn billions of people to enforced and permanent misery at precisely the moment when their liberation is in sight. Unfortunately, most people still think in the concepts of the first Industrial Revolution. They see that we have more and better machines than fifty years ago and mark this down as progress. The progress achieved in technology gives the illusion that people are steadily progressing in the political, moral, cultural, and sociological areas as well. But the expression and fulfillment of human potentialities requires a different approach from that based solely on the control of natural forces. To the extent that technology ignores fundamental insights into the nature of man, it may become an agent of regression. Many analysts are deeply concerned that technology has created a civilization that is producing change faster than society can understand it or control it.[12]

Whereas the Agricultural Revolution took millennia and the Industrial Revolution required centuries, the Scientific Revolution is measured by the generation. We are so accustomed to rapid social change that it is easy to believe that science is unlimited in its capacity to create new knowledge. In many important ways, technology does feed on itself and tends to improve despite the fluctuations of other patterns. But man is, after all, a biological organism with a limited ability to absorb the various stresses and strains inherent in the tempo of rapid change. Moreover, in some fields there is only a limited potential for the creation of new knowledge. There are definite limitations on the changes that technology can produce.

Granted that technological progress in this century has outstripped all predictions and expectations, the future may well be devoted to a period of consolidation and clarification. There are, of course, areas where new growth and development are essential; there are other areas which should be leveled off or cut back. We can predict with a great deal of confidence that technology will change and that all existing political and economic institutions will undergo some modifications as a result of this new technology. Along with the revolution in communications, transportation, and standards of living, we can also expect profound changes in the educational process. Technological advancement is no longer simply that of increasing the productivity of machines. If man is passive in the face of his technology, he may also be apathetic and abdicate his moral responsibility with regard to the humane uses of technological advances.

The technological society requires trained intelligence but it also requires moral qualities and ethical decisions. Technology stands in the very center of present-day culture. The spectacular advances in basic science which have produced man's accelerating technology have given him enormous control over his environment. As the man-made sectors of the human environment grow in importance, technology more and more partakes of the nature of man. The urge to alter and improve the conditions of life is clearly a basic human instinct. Technology has spawned all kinds of artificial environments that encompass our everyday lives. As technology advances, each step involves a new mode of thinking to relate to the actuality of the new environment that is created.[13] The future of man will be greatly affected by his ability to adapt to the new environments that are being created.

The ambivalence of technology grows with its increasing complexity. It is wise for us to question continually whether we are using tools or becoming subservient to them. Erich Fromm writes:

> The first principle of the technological society
> is the maxim that something ought to be done
> because it is technically possible to do it. This
> principle means the negation of all values which the
> humanist tradition has developed. This tradition
> said that something should be done because it
> is needed for man, for his growth, joy, and reason,
> because it is beautiful, good, or true. Once the
> principle is accepted that something ought to be
> done because it is technically possible to do it,
> all other values are dethroned and technological
> development becomes the foundation of ethics.[14]

The scientific-technological complex that has functioned so well during the past century will continue to produce more of the same by its own momentum. But the present emphasis on assessing technology is an encouraging sign that people are considering goals to be as important as means in the development of a technological civilization. Among the hopeful signs of the times is the growing concern with the quality of life as a main criterion of success. The resistance to purely materialistic growth goals is a sign that concern for the good life is not dead and that human will can overcome technological power. There is increasing dissatisfaction with official priorities that degrade the quality and meaning of life.

Changing technology plainly alters the means available to the individual and society for attaining value derived goals. When we apply new modes of technology to traditional value achievement situations, the values themselves may change subtly. Put another way, technology changes the framework of value satisfaction. Pleasure, beauty, wealth, and power can be defined quite differently according to the technological framework in which they are situated. Thus scientific technology requires society to make ethical decisions. Recent developments in pharmacology and neurophysiology has focused attention on technological possibilities for controlling behavior and changing personality in radical ways. Systematic applications of such techniques would have broad social implications. Developments that are taking place in the field of genetics indicate a future where at least some of the aspects of evolution and a great deal of genetic planning will be in human hands. Biology is now at the very center of scientific activity; its recent and probable future discoveries have the most profound implications for the human race.

Mankind stands at the threshold of understanding how genes operate in building and maintaining the human organism. Genetic engineering is becoming a casually accepted term: some scientists speak eagerly of "the design of the man of the future." A Harvard zoologist has stated that man can undergo important evolutionary changes in ten generations or less.[15] Thus in three hundred years significant alterations may be made in the emotional and intellectual traits of mankind. Dr. Robert L. Sinsheimer of the California Institute of Technology argues that genetics has reached a state similar to that of atomic physics in the 1930s. He speculates that

> we will surely come to the time when man will have the power to alter, specifically and consciously, his very genes. This will be a new event in the universe. No longer need nature wait for the chance mutation and the slow process of selection. Intelligence can be applied to evolution. How might we like to change his genes? Perhaps we would like to alter the uneasy balance of our emotions. Should we become less warlike, more self-confident, more serene? Perhaps we shall finally achieve these long-sought goals with techniques far superior to those with which we have had to make do for centuries.[16]

The main fear associated with these research areas is that, once sufficient knowledge is gained, techniques will become available that will allow men to manipulate other men. To prescribe the genetic constitution of the man of the future is to claim to know what the ideal human being ought to be like. This is not biology but ethics and moral philosophy. We must always ask: What legitimates the moral concerns of the scientist who will carry out these experiments and programs? What are their values? The control of the destiny of man through this knowledge is fraught with the political dangers of tyranny and the social dangers of dehumanization. Genetic control touches man at his most intimate levels and raises the specters of totalitarian manipulation reminiscent of *Brave New World* and *1984*. A strictly scientific view of man might tend to regard society as a vast laboratory in which only the genetic manipulator and his political masters retain their freedom. Human equality is an ethical precept, not a biological phenomenon. A society can grant or withhold it from its members. The caste system in India was the grandest genetic experiment ever performed on man. The structure of the society attempted for more than two millennia to induce genetic specialization of the caste populations for performance of different types of work and functions.[17]

The writings of Professor H. J. Muller give the most vivid portrayal of the genetic dilemmas into which the human race is heading.[18] Among other things, Professor Muller advocates the establishment of sperm banks and mass artificial insemination of women (whose husbands, presumably, do not consider their own genes worthy of being passed on to their progeny). The sperm of great men would be maintained in frozen form for many years and be made available for the fathering of children by many mothers. A little imagination suggests some fantastic scenarios involving genetic manipulation on a mass scale. For example, will the United States, China, and the Soviet Union embark on a genetics race comparable to the armaments races of today? Among some geneticists there is a strong conviction that they know what the ideal human types are and therefore the world should gladly follow their prescriptions.

Dr. Viktor Frankl has written that the gas chambers of Auschwitz were a consequence of the theory that man is nothing but the product of heredity and environment.[19] H. J. Muller had supreme confidence that those pioneers in the employment of germinal selection could be trusted to choose the types that would be good for mankind to produce in greatest numbers. But we could observe a science that strikes at the very roots of human society, putting an end to the biological diversity that has done so much to enrich the life of man. Such control of man on a society-wide scale could be extremely dangerous unless the scientists were constantly aware that the men they seek to control are human beings and not like the inanimate objects of engineering in the laboratory. The choices are staggering. Who will make the decisions? Who will assume the responsibility for errors?

The genetic revolution which is now before us implies that our biological foundation is no longer subject simply to natural selection of the fittest. The time to review new technologies is before they are implemented; scientists and technologists cannot ignore the fact that they add to the burden of a society already overwhelmed by the need to manage its fate and to make many serious choices about the future. Until recently, science has been largely engaged in modifying the environment to suit man; now we have arrived at a point where science is capable of modifying man to suit his environment. What is crucial is that one set of men will be intervening in the lives of other people, determining the traits of other people's children, and presenting "parents" with children not of their own "procreation." When men begin to exercise such power over other men, they leave the laboratory behind them and enter the political arena. Any application of this knowledge will take place within the existing sociopolitical framework of power and privilege. Will the objects of such social engineering turn out to be the poor and the powerless, presumably of "inferior" stock? The political process in large measure determines the uses of science; moreover, when the scientist projects social goals he is invariably going to project his own cultural prejudices.

Those who are studying the impact of the new technologies agree that man must anticipate his future if that future is to have any meaning. Yet a great deal of current study and planning continues to be based on the assumption that our future will resemble the past. A question now being posed to contemporary civilization is: Out of all the possible futures toward which man can direct his continuing evolution, which ones does he really desire? Today, almost any kind of future is technically within his reach. The rapid expansion of the range of human alternatives means that many difficult choices must be made. Speaking of the importance of choice in modern life, Professor David Apter has written:

> To be modern means to see life as alternatives,
> preferences, and choices. Self-conscious choice
> implies rationality. Men will in principle see more
> than one alternative as plausible. Preferences
> include the ranking of priorities, and about these
> reasonable men may differ. One of the
> characteristics of the modernization process is that
> it involves both aspects of choice: the
> improvement of the conditions of choice, and the
> selection of the most satisfactory mechanisms
> of choice.[20]

The most important point about these consequences

of technological development is that they in turn have their own consequences; that is, individually and collectively they require adjustments in the social system. Until fairly recently in human history, only a minority had the chance to develop their full personality. The historical values of Western civilization have adapted themselves to many forms of revolutionary change. There is no reason why they cannot survive the enormous transitions that will inevitably take place as we conclude the twentieth century.

MODERN TECHNOLOGY AND HUMAN VALUES

The belief in progress, in man's ability to master his problems and change life for the better, has been shattered by the course of twentieth-century events. For all those who believe in progress as an ideal of action, the course of recent history has brought bitter disillusionment. Everywhere there are doubts as to the solidity of our political, economic, and social structures. The new element is a profound pessimism that we shall have the capacity to master our problems. The most naturally optimistic people in the world are beginning to wonder whether events are, indeed, out of control. The earlier notions of inevitable progress have been shaken. The "Armageddon syndrome" envisions a host of intractable problems that will torment man and subject him to terrible pressures.[21] The energy crisis, the apparently unstoppable inflation that we see in every industrialized capitalist nation, the man-made ecological imbalances, the outbreaks of violence and irrationalism, the loss of privacy and solitude, the loss of human scale and perspective, the growth of dangerously vulnerable technology systems, and the pronounced tendencies toward a hedonistic, selfish culture pose questions having the most profound implications for the future of our society.[22]

Since the Renaissance, and especially since the nineteenth century, progress has been seen as desirable, inevitable, and beneficial. As we have seen, this notion of progress was very closely linked with a view of technological and material progress. But this century differs from the nineteenth in the accelerating pace of change, the wide-ranging ramifications of machine practices and techniques, and the influence of these on every aspect of life and thought. We are constantly being battered by the cumulative consequences of something we hardly knew we were doing. As a result, the range of choice and the degree of conscious control which man may exercise in determining his future are unprecedented.[23] The irony is that in the face of such extraordinary opportunities the feelings of pessimism have never been greater. We are witnessing an understandable reaction against the blithe faith in progress that was in fashion in the nineteenth century. But the new antifaith that seeks to portray the unique alienation of modern man is as unsound and simplistic as the old faith in progress.

It is now intellectually fashionable to cast a gloomy eye toward the future. In fact, despondency and pessimism are so fashionable nowadays that to suggest a more hopeful prospect seems philistine. Broadly speaking, we are told that man is a failure and that science and technology are the archvillains responsible for much of his unhappiness. Curiously, the same prophets of doom who have lost the belief in man's rationality and look askance at the fruits of science and technology maintain one kind of optimism: their faith in our capacity to foresee the future. When it comes to forecasting various disasters, they claim to possess a rather startling prescience. This confidence seems strange because of all the notions the optimistic era advanced, the idea that we can accurately predict the future is among those least supported by our past experience.

In any event, such morose pontification is based on an extremely limited selection among the facts of our time. The full view of the facts would appear to provide a valid justification for exhilaration rather than despair. This is certainly not to imply that all the criticism of science and technology as used by human beings today is invalid or undeserved, nor that much good may result from the various critiques of our scientific-technological civilization. The feedback from such criticism can be fruitfully absorbed and the best of it will have a valuable effect on our society. However, in the current attempts to weigh the benefits of technology against its risks, the critics often ask for the impossible; namely, scientific answers to questions that are trans-scientific. What the scientist can do in clarifying matters of trans-science differs from what he can do in clarifying matters of science. Western science operates within strict boundaries, concerning itself with the limitation and control of variables. No such clarity is possible for human affairs in general. A social system derives from a staggering number of variables; we can rarely discover which are most important. Scientists sometimes refuse to concede that science has limits. The debate on risks versus benefits would be more fruitful if we recognized these limits.[24]

In their impatience with the various imperfections of our society, a great many of our contemporary intellectuals tend to forget the enormous progress made possible by the development of science and technology. Both science and technology are, and always have been, integral to the human adventure. They have contributed to our humanity, and to view them as alien to the concerns of the human race would be palpably absurd. On balance, one is compelled to say that the advances in technology already made and to be made promise that mankind's future can be much brighter than its past. We must never forget that the mass of mankind today still lives in a prescientific, preindustrial society. If man were to pursue the illusion that he could adjust to nature without a constant upgrading of his science and technology, he would soon become extinct. Far from crushing and dehumanizing human beings, technology has created a society of such complex diversity and richness that its members have a greater range of personal choice and a more highly developed sense of personal worth than ever before.

Of course, in many ways the twentieth-century technological revolution has just begun. The major problem confronting society now is how to reap all the advantages that technology has to offer while at the same time overcoming the negative consequences of technological progress. The unintended consequences of achievements that are good in themselves are an inescapable fact of the human condition. Daniel Callahan points out:

> One price of progress is the substitution of new problems for old. That mankind seems willing to pay it does not make the new problems any less real, or fearsome. The advances of medicine, technology, and the life sciences have meant, among other things, a lowering of infant mortality rates, the gradual conquest of disease and disabilities, a longer life expectancy and the possibility of family limitation and population

the creative use of leisure time. Almost certainly there will have to be mass re-education to show people how their leisure can be most creatively employed.

The accelerating advance of technology is moving us toward a novel state of society. The issues of work and leisure mushroom into an endless progression of questions.[33] Already, there are indications that the willingness to work is declining in some sectors of industrial society. Bored automobile workers have been known to sabotage their assembly lines; corporate executives have "dropped out" from the pressures of the executive suite; there is widespread alienation among youth with regard to current conditions of work that is regarded as unfulfilling or soul-destroying. But problems of boredom and lack of personal fulfillment will not disappear with increasing automation and the advent of more free time. George Bernard Shaw warned that "unlimited leisure is a definition of Hell." The Puritan ethic has prepared us for work, not leisure— and to many people the activities of leisure do not extend beyond beer, bowling, and boating. An extraordinary number of people find their identity and sense of worth in their work; to be released from such work is more appalling than appealing.

The ideal solution is a world in which technology is used for human purposes and life and work are integrated into a productive, self-fulfilling abundance. This is not an impossible dream. We do not lack resources: the recovery of confidence is within our grasp if we reassert humanistic values and seek the restoration of ethical norms in human enterprise. As René Dubos has pointed out, man has been driven by the conviction that he can and should transform the world to make it a better and happier place.[34] Man is essentially an ideal-forming creature; the formation of ideals is an indispensable element in his progress. The crucial factor is that men *act* as though they believe in the possibility of progress for mankind, even when they disagree on the interpretation of the significance of various technical advances. Throughout its history, the human species has been preoccupied with the conquest of nature and the control of environment. Practically all aspects of human life are artificial in the sense that they depend on profound modifications of the natural order of things. Human beings choose to be human by changing the world around them to suit their basic natures; precisely because we are human animals we cannot trust to chance. The human species prospers primarily by choices. If modern man hungers for values beyond those of the megamachine, he must remember that the human being has always been the starting point for new effects. What lies ahead for civilization is obviously more complex than the conditions that confronted earlier social systems. Whatever else he may be, man has been simultaneously a problem-creating and problem-solving creature. How fundamental and lasting the revolt against technology will become in contemporary Western culture can only be conjectured. The future will tell whether man will recoil from the abuses of technology and deliberately curtail its advancement. We have seen that it is no easy matter to use technology for the promotion of human values.

Technology has given man unprecedented control over his environment; it has also given him unprecedented responsibilities. Past generations have tended to worship economic growth and productivity. It is the emphasis on productivity as a self-justifying end that must be altered if we are to humanize the fruits of technology. We can be the best-clothed, best-fed, best-housed people in the world and the most unhappy people without the higher goals and values that give our society a sense of purpose and direction.[35] The most pressing need for twentieth-century man is transforming the outmoded industrial paradigm and creating a social order more in conformity with environmental imperatives. A civilization reveals the nature of its goals and values in the environmental conditions that it creates. The development of a humane civilization depends upon goal-directed institutions capable of using science and technology so as to create environments which are favorable to the continued growth of civilization.[36]

A better civilization remains to be created. The idea that human nature is incapable of improvement and that the ideals of Judeo-Christian civilization must be adjusted to human nature at its most mediocre must be rejected if the framework of a better civilization is to be created. The solution to current problems will not be found in a retreat from the Judeo-Christian tradition or from technological civilization. Instead, an ethic adequate to man's responsibility for the whole earth must be created within that framework. Can there be moral progress? Can men and women become better than they are? Can a technological civilization create a culture that encourages the individual in his efforts to make a good life for himself and his family? The politics of the last four decades should have taught us that government cannot cope with the crisis of values that is sweeping the Western world. Government cannot provide values to persons who have none; it cannot provide inner peace or a meaning to life.[37] Nor is morality to be found in the latest public opinion polls (equating the morally good with what the crowd wants and tolerates). Robert J. Steamer speaks to this point most eloquently:

> Disorder in today's society is, in part, the result of our rejection of any permanent, transcending values, of our insistence that there is no higher law, no higher reality outside ourselves. Unless we return to the concept that standards of decency and civility are something more than personal preferences, we shall remain in a state of moral anarchy in which the degrading and the ennobling have equal status, a state in which appeals will be made in the name of freedom to the worst in all of us.[38]

Scientific technology, presenting mankind with new possibilities for the enhancement or destruction of life, requires society to make careful ethical decisions. Power implies responsibilities, both social and moral. Technology can no longer be taken for granted; it must be continually assessed if it is to be employed for humane purposes. The effort to make technology the scapegoat of all our social ills is a vast oversimplification; being "against" the increase of potentialities afforded by technological progress seems fatuous. Membership in a technologically advanced and advancing society is a privilege; it is characteristic of all privileges that they may be put to good use or bad use.[39]

Technology as a human phenomenon is here to stay. The essential task of our time is to arrive at an understanding of technology which will neither idolize nor condemn it, but rather be able to elucidate its positive values while perceiving its possible hazards.[40] However bitter our disillusionment with man and society has been in recent years, there are valid reasons for believing that we do really progress and that we can continue to achieve change for the better with the restoration of a sound moral philosophy to serve as a lodestone for our basic human yearnings. Technological feats that interfere with fundamental human yearnings must be resisted. Obviously, not all directions are good for human happiness and moral goodness. The notion that we *should* do something because we *can* do it is both operationally and ethically meaningless. It seems beyond dispute that certain powers are dangerous, certain inventions are threats rather than promises. The previously discussed risks involved in programming human heredity are an excellent case in point. Moral and ethical considerations weigh as heavily as biological ones in determining whether such steps should be taken. If such innovations are attempted, resulting in a future society which holds human life less sacred than in the past, the end result could spell moral and social catastrophe. We cannot afford to have the cancer of moral decay gnawing away at the body of science. To postulate "gains" achieved by the flagrant disregard of human rights is intolerable.

Father Walter Ong has provided an optimistic answer to those who tremble at the thought of the future "technological man." He writes:

> The age of technology is part of the great and mysterious evolution of the universe devised by God. It can be considered as an epoch in what we may call the hominization of the world; that is, the taking over of our planet by mankind.[41]

It is said that after the ceremonies dedicating the great

Mount Palomar telescope, an onlooker remarked to an astronomer: "Modern astronomy certainly makes man look insignificant, doesn't it?" To which the astronomer replied, "But man is the astronomer!" It is not only human to invent; it is also human to keep moving toward a destination which realizes the highest aspirations of man. In the future, the very survival of mankind may depend on our constructing an edifice of civilization such as never existed before. We must behave in more civilized ways than our ancestors. The creation of the conditions of civilized living is a never-ending task. The greater our material power, the greater our need for spiritual insight and virtue to use that power for good and not for evil. For material power that is not balanced by spiritual insight (that is, by wisdom and love) is a curse. If civilization is to survive, the coming age must be one of spiritual as well as social integration. To make the hominization of the world a reality, our technological culture must become rooted in altruism and the most sublime ideals of conduct. Technology now confronts us with profound questions of human value. The human species is gradually seeking its goal and fulfilling its destiny: the discovery of truth and the creation of a better world for those who will follow after us.

chapter II

David J. Hassel, S.J., Ph.D.

Progress and Crisis in Secular Values

No one doubts that the world is going through the paroxysms of a vast social change. Many scholars are convinced that the secularization process is the catalyst promoting this revolution. But few are able to define this process to their own or their colleagues' satisfaction. In the final panel discussion at the University of Notre Dame Colloquium on Secularity, Professor Wilfred Cantwell Smith, director of the Center for the Study of World Religions at Harvard University, expressed the frustration of the twenty-five scholar participants: "The point which I should above all carry away from this discussion is the firm resolve never to use the word 'secularity' again. It appears to be a term of utter confusion."[1] In response to Professor Smith a person could ask: "But if we do not work toward a clearer understanding of the terms 'secularity' and 'secularization,' how can there be a just estimate of where the present worldwide social change is heading?"

What is particularly puzzling in this confused situation is that each expert seems to have two definitions of the secularization process. One appears abstract and philosophic; the other is concrete and historical. For example, according to Larry Shiner, Friedrich Gogarten, the pioneer German theologian of the secular, describes secularization as "the transformation of institutions, ideas, and experiences that were once the work of divine providence into the product of purely human thought and action."[2] This is a more concrete and historical description than the more philosophical Gogarten definition of secularization as "the transformation of the relation between man and the world from a mythical unity with the cosmos to responsibility for the world."[3]

Again, Jacques Maritain starkly etches historical secularization as the progressive severance of earthly civilization from evangelical inspiration, while admitting that in itself secularization is a process of distinction for a better form of union[4] (i.e., a process of specialization leading to a greater socialization). Apparently for Maritain this neutral, perhaps even good, process turned out historically to be a bitter tragedy.

It is noteworthy that the sociologist Robert Nisbet defines secularization (amid three other major processes of change: individualization, innovation, politicization) in historical terms as "the passage of sacred norms into secular, the replacement of a social order largely governed by religious values by one in which utilitarian or secular values are dominant."[5] However, whenever he wishes to speak with essential clarity, he turns to Max Weber's handy philosophic definition of secularization as the rationalization typical of Greek thought and modern systematic science.

Edward Schillebeeckx, the prominent theologian, seems particularly aware of this distinction between levels of discourse. He first describes secularization in Weberian terms as the discovery of man's rational sphere of understanding. But then he adds that this same process is a sociohistorical phenomenon in which the world and human society are so conceived within this rational sphere of understanding that they are gradually withdrawn from the tutelage of the Church and of religion.[6]

Why do these thinkers feel the need to give a double definition of secularization? Is it possible that the philosophic definition refers more to the causal elements interior to secularization and that the sociohistoric definition looks more to the exterior effects of secularization? Is it possible that behind these definitions is a common understanding which can reveal how all these insightful definitions converge to explain the vast social change now occurring throughout the world? Would it be impertinent to try to move toward such a common understanding of secularization?

In order to respond to these questions through the following pages, it will be necessary to map out how the secularization process is traveling within the organization of communities and throughout the lives of the individual members of these communities. This will give us a provisional definition of what is meant by secularization taken philosophically. Such a definition can then be related to all the previous definitions in order to see whether or not it may implicitly underlie each of them as their common understanding. This is our first step.

Once secularization taken philosophically is recognizable with some clarity, it will be easier, in a second step, to distinguish it from the secularity which always accompanies it and from the secularism which falsely claims to be the secularization process itself.

With these three pervasive and mutually modifying factors of culture carefully disentangled, it will be possible, in a third step, to see how each operates within so many of our civic problems ranging from servant-class poverty and establishment bigness to racism and technological depersonalization.

Finally, after all this, some tentative conclusions can be drawn concerning the use of secularization and secularity to measure human progress amid the continuing crises of man.

TOWARD A COMMON UNDERSTANDING OF SECULARIZATION
Communal Specialization and
Integration (Socialization)

If one looks long enough at the central factors of civilization such as education, government, business, religion, family life, labor unions, the military, the entertainment industry, and so on, one is struck by the rapidity with which each has specialized its activities, procedures, and institutions and then integrated or socialized them all into a more complex unity. The twin processes of specialization (diversification) and integration (socialization), in mutually advancing each other, swiftly expand the organization in which they occur.

For example, if a person compares a university catalogue for 1925 with one for 1975, he discovers not only new sciences within a traditional scientific field like biology (e.g., genetics, gerontology, microbiology, biophysics) but also whole new scientific fields such as cybernetics and human engineering. Specialization, here taken as the discovery of new knowledges, is luxuriant. But it could be destructive if it were not balanced, controlled, and directed by the alternative process of integration, which in this case would be the unifying of these knowledges. Such integrative unifying occurs when a particular problem demands the use of many of these knowledges for its solution. Thus, the problem of environmental pollution requires first that scientists converge the physical sciences of physics, biology, chemistry, and meteorology on the purely physical aspects of pollution; and second, that they focus the social sciences of psychology, history, anthropology, economics, and sociology on the human aspects of the problem. Meanwhile philosophers and theologians will be cooperating to discover the moral context and radical motivation for solving this problem.

In order to work toward solving the problem of pollution, the various scientists must cooperatively integrate their knowledges. The biochemist and the physical chemist must relate their findings concerning mercury in man's diet to the psychologist's discovery of anxiety and depression in those undergoing mercury poisoning. At the same time, the economist, sociologist, chemical engineer, and political scientist work to develop a fair assessment of industrial responsibility and to devise the means for making the dumping of mercury into public waters unnecessary as well as unlawful. Using the data gathered by the physical and social scientists as a guide, philosophers outline how the very dignity of man requires that he find a solution to the problem of mercury-dumping—a solution which will promote man's environment. Theologians, in turn, employing the scientific data and the philosophic principles, will show in faith how such development of man's environment can contribute to the development of God's people. In thus cooperatively weaving their knowledges into a single pattern of understanding, these scholars are beginning to create a great tapestry of world vision.

For each one of these knowledges is now better seen because it has been fitted into a context of other knowledges, has been indirectly corrected by them, and has been stimulated to take new approaches to its own data.

Because of the complexity of the world and because of his own limitations of intelligence, will, imagination, and sheer physical energy, man has been forced to specialize; that is, to concentrate his efforts and to delimit the questions he asks of reality. If a single genius attempted to know the whole universe scientifically, he would at best merely penetrate its surface and discover that "playing God" is fruitless, not to say dangerous. But by concentrating, e.g., within sociology, on the attitudes of Midwest urban Slavic minorities, he can go ever more deeply into a small area of reality. Such specialization, when later allied with other similar specializations, not only produces an overall vision of some depth but also challenges each of the specialists to return to his specialty with sharpened vision for deeper probing. Our sociologist, confronted with the diverse findings on other racial minorities both in the United States and Europe, now has the expanded and balanced vision to see more clearly the Slavic minority of the urban Midwest. In this way, integration or socialization dialectically demands further specialization, which in turn requires a new and deeper integration if it is to escape narrowness and warping.

All that has been said about knowledges and their practitioners in the university is, with some differences, just as true in government, business, religion, labor unions, the armed forces, the entertainment world, and so on. Note the proliferation of government agencies to meet the more and more specialized problems of low-rental city housing, agriculture lag, law enforcement, foreign trade deficit, and diplomatic complexities. And within each of these agencies, committees are multiplying in order to face the many facets of each developing problem. More and more, the need for coordinating agencies into integrated programs is being felt. Specialization without concomitant integration leads gradually to chaos. Business with its conglomerates, the church with its hierarchies of officials and committees, the labor unions with their members, the entertainment and publishing industries with their interlocking connections into all civic and educational areas, the armed forces with their complex technology of weaponry, supply logistics, and training—all these factors of civilization are becoming swiftly aware of the constant need for reintegration within themselves and along with the other factors of civilization.

Individual Specialization and
Integration (Socialization)

At this point, it might be well to ask, What effect does all this communal specialization and integration (socialization) have on the individual person? First of all, it should be clear that these twin processes must first be operative within the individual community members before they can be exteriorized and maintained in and by some community organization. To exemplify this, recall the experience of the collegian who is overwhelmed by the variety of diverse approaches made by literature, history, psychology, sociology, philosophy, theology, biology, and anthropology to the meaning of man. To avoid being rendered distraught by seemingly contradictory statements about man, the undergraduate must, bit by bit, integrate the findings of these knowledges into the whole of his personal experience. Specialization could dice his consciousness into small, distracting, unattached bits unless integration accompanies all of the diversification.

Indeed, the consoles of instrumentation facing the airline pilot or the modern truck driver as they mount into the cockpit or cab symbolize the remarkable specialization demanded of each. The expert conduct of the air flight or the transport testifies to the individual integration of each expert. But this is only part of his integration; he is probably also a union member, a father, a husband, a member of a church. Somehow, within a man, all the knowledges and attitudes and skills needed to perform all these functions must be coordinated so that he leads one life and not multiple, anxiety-ridden, possibly schizoid lives.

This specialization and integration interior to the individual man explains how it is possible for an airline company or a transport workers union or a government agency or a church or an army to come into existence and survive. The more specialized the knowledge of the individual, the better able he is to carry out the highly specialized work of his company or union and to cooperate with other specialists. But a man is no longer just a farmer or an airline pilot; he must support a number of diverse organizations such as his family, union, church, political party, bowling team, and so on. He must have specialized knowledges and skills other than his work-skill so that he can support and direct these other organizations.

Further, he must have them integrated within himself since too much interest in the labor union may undermine his skill as an airline pilot, too much involvement in church and political affairs may render him a poor father and husband. And failure as husband-father can result in failure as pilot and union man. The balance of his skills and attitudes—an always readjusting balance—will determine how helpful he can be to all communities and organizations in which he works. Therefore the higher the quality of his integration, the more effective will be his specialization. The reverse is also true: the more professionally competent the airline pilot becomes, the more highly respected and consequently effective he will be in his union and, perhaps, in his family.

Because professional competence arises out of specialization and integration (socialization) which are at once individual and communal, it is no surprise that knowledge- and skill-communities define with exceeding care their special areas of competence, set up criteria for membership, and establish controls for ensuring work quality. The amateur electrician is just as dangerous as the amateur hospital dietitian; both endanger the physical and psychological health not only of the civic community but also of the specialist community itself.

Provisional Definition of Secularization

From these examples, perhaps a definition of secularization can be tentatively drawn. It appears to be a human process whereby knowledges, skills, and their serving community members are differentiated or specialized. Thus areas and rules of competence become more defined in such a way as to exploit and protect these knowledges and their serving communities. As a result, these communities, through interdependent cooperative activity, can expand, enrich, and unite not only their knowledges and skills but also themselves, the national community, and even the international community. This last aspect is the dialectical integration or socialization correlative with specialization.

Secularization, then, as found in the individual, is actually the expansion of his personality around a specialized skill or knowledge. As the latter develops, it roots the skilled person more deeply in the community, enables him to grow more skillful through service to the community, and gives him a fuller sense of contributing to the wider communities through integration of his skill or knowledge with the diverse skills or knowledges of other specialists. Thus secularization becomes for the individual a deeper and deeper penetration into the world and its various communities, through a deeper and deeper experience and service within his skill- or knowledge-community. Further, the differentiation or specialization of the individual's personality demands higher integration. The latter, in turn, calls for more differentiation, since successfully integrated service to the community increases the desire to serve better through greater, i.e., more specialized, skill.

Therefore, secularization, taken communally, is an expansion of the collective personality of the community whose skill, in penetrating reality more deeply and effectively, renders it more capable of serving other communities and cooperating with them in common endeavors. Again, the differentiation or specialization of the collective personality demands integration or socialization which is both the cooperation of these specialized communities in some common product and the resultant ties of coordinated techniques, knowledges, and friendships. The collaborative building of a model town by architects, engineers, the building trades, landscapers, philosophers, government agencies, bankers, merchants, and many other groups illustrates this point.

It becomes clearer at this juncture that secularization is a deeper and deeper penetration of reality, both personal and infrapersonal. This naturally results in a deeper and deeper dedication to the universe of physical elements, plants, animals and men—a dedication which does not necessarily exclude a Reality which is immanent to and yet beyond the universe. Such a process of growing union with the whole world is well termed "secularization."

The centrality of Weber's statement that secularization is rationalization becomes more evident when one notes how the previous description of this process reveals conceptualization (knowledge and skill development) working at the dynamic core of the secularization process. Secularization happened because, in contradistinction to the mythic, concrete, imaginative, personal approach to reality, the Greeks began to develop an alternate procedure characterized as abstract, conceptual, and impersonal. This latter eventually became what we now call "science."[7] The resultant scientific concepts were found to be highly maneuverable, analyzable into significant parts, and applicable to a wide diversity of circumstances apart from geography, time, custom, and particular attitudes.

Later, in the medieval period, the remnants of the Greek conceptual schemes were to develop the technology of sextant, water mill, optical devices, distilling of liquids, and so on, so that concepts became allied to techniques, routines, and procedures and enabled the latter to be passed on by way of books rather than by long-term

apprenticeships of practice.[8] Though this scientific conceptualization was already the secularization process in operation, still this process was notably accelerated when
these conceptualizations took shape in visible machines,
agricultural techniques, manufacturing procedures, and
distilling routines. For then the latter became more specialized through improved techniques and in this way helped
to perfect or specialize the accompanying conceptualization. The modern invention of the Ford assembly line is a
good example of this. It incarnates not merely the latest
discoveries of chemistry and physics but also those of economics, psychology and human engineering. The worker
may not reflectively know all of the concepts involved,
but he lives them. As a result he becomes a specialized
skill worker; and the Ford car, in its turn, "lives" these
concepts. Further, the worker's association with others on
the assembly line eventually produces the auto workers'
union, a set of attitudes characteristic of the Detroit auto
worker, and, perhaps, a softball team. All this incarnates
Weber's theory of rationalization. Clearly, Schillebeeckx's
definition of secularization as the discovery of man's rational sphere of understanding fits neatly the developing
pattern of our investigation.

These examples also illustrate Gogarten's contention
that secularization is the transformation of man's attitude
toward the world from mythical union to personal responsibility. For, although man cannot live well without
a poetic imaginative embracing of the world, still he cannot support the present population of the world without
taking on a scientific responsibility for tilled lands, open
skies, teeming oceans, industrial complexes, aggressive gov-
ernments, and religious understandings and living. Man
no longer relies merely on literature, liturgy, familial love,

and time-worn traditions of farming and trade skills. He also must employ pragmatic and highly conceptualized techniques, bureaucracies, and organizations.[9]

The very complexity of these organizations with their interlocking cooperations demands that the individual worker be allowed freedom to adapt his specialized skill to the needs of the moment. Such freedom correlatively demands of the worker a higher degree of responsibility —a responsibility multiplied by the number of communities to which he belongs and contributes. Now this responsibility is precisely his ability to integrate his own personality around his skills and obligations and to express this integration through his specialized skills. Thus individual responsible integration is expanded into communal responsible integration (socialization).[10]

Here Gogarten's and Weber's definitions together with our previous description of secularization are seen stripped to their inner core by Maritain's philosophic definition: a process of distinction for a better form of union. Here, too, the introduction of the word "better" would seem to imply that secularization is at least the measure of progress if not progress itself.

Obviously, in showing the convergence of these "more philosophic" definitions around individual and communal differentiation (specialization) and socialization (integration), one whole set of definitions was omitted, the socio-historical. Behind this procedure are two convictions: (1) that a philosophic understanding underlies all the other understandings of secularization[11]; and (2) that the socio-historical definitions actually refer to something distinctly other than secularization yet operative within secularization, namely *secularity* or value-system.

Some explanation for these convictions is necessary.

In the first place, the very fact that our single philosophic definition of secularization proved to be explanatory of the "more philosophic" definitions offered by Nisbet, Weber, Gogarten, and Maritain, would indicate that our definition is a central understanding of the secularization process. Now the secondary "more socio-historical" definition of each of these experts is derivative from his primary "more philosophic" definition. To take the example of Gogarten—it is because man has become more scientifically responsible for the world and less mythically united with the cosmos that man has transformed his institutions, ideas, and experience from being merely the work of divine providence to being the product of purely human thought and action. To take Nisbet's description of secularization—it is because man has developed reasoned systems of scientific thought explanatory of the universe to its outer limits and explanatory of man to his innermost depths that a social order dominated by utilitarian secular values has replaced an order largely governed by religious values. Thus, if the "more socio-historic" definitions of these experts are derived from their "more philosophic" definitions and if our definition serves to converge and to explain their "more philosophic" definitions, then we have good reason to think that our single definition underlies and explains all these definitions.

In the second place, note that the socio-historic definitions emphasize values and norms more than the particular conceptual systems which differentiate or specialize knowledges, skills, and their serving communities. This emphasis would point to a second cultural factor: value systems (which we shall call *secularities*). To confuse these two distinct factors would seem to introduce exasperating confusion into one's thought and life. For, if one fails to distinguish between actions and the motives (or values) which direct these actions, one risks either phariseeism where a person puts all the emphasis on fulfilling routines no matter the value, or hypocrisy where a person takes little care to integrate his valued ideals with his behavior.

Consequently, secularity, any value system for living deeply in the world, may possibly, by its very distinctness from secularization, be more a response to secularization than the inner meaning of the latter. That is, secularity may be more a set of resultant attitudes for redirecting secularization rather than the process itself.[12] But in the complex socio-historical context, the response could be easily confused with its stimulus; while the attitudes or values first resultant of, and later reciprocally directive of, secularization could blend almost imperceptibly with secularization. These possibilities must be considered. Otherwise, it will be difficult to discover (1) whether or not the secularization process is itself cultural progress (and therefore a major factor in this decade's wide and deep social changes) and (2) whether or not secularity is a cultural factor distinct from the secularization process (and therefore is a second index for cultural progress).

SECULARIZATION—NEITHER SECULARITY NOR SECULARISM
Secularity

It seems that individual and communal personality expansion cannot occur without a concomitant rising of values or attitudes toward one's own special skill or knowledge, toward the diverse skills and knowledges of other community-servants, toward the evolving world, and toward God (who is rather persistently charged with starting the world and with interfering in its workings). For, is it not true that a person must learn to value his special skill or knowledge if he is to suffer long the discipline necessary for its maintenance and growth? Further, when he cooperates with other skilled and knowledgeable men and women, does he not learn how to evaluate his own knowledge or skill by locating its position of relative importance within the project? In doing this, must not a man or woman take a stand on what the world, personal and infrapersonal, is worth and where it is going? Neighborhood, national, and international communities seem to be weighed in this balance of values—at least implicitly. Eventually, too, does not man have to take a position on whether or not there is a controlling presence throughout the universe and whether, if there is one, this presence is personal and benevolent?[13]

How the individual sets up his constellation of leading values would, then, appear to determine how he cooperates within the secularization process, since his values become attitudes and the latter run or ruin the world. Is it not our experience that within the specialist community a collective set of values begins to arise from the individual members and to reinforce the values of each individual? Does this not set the tonal quality of the work done by this community? In addition, does not this collective value system begin to qualify the value systems of other cooperating specialist communities so that eventually a national set of values starts to surface?

Let us take a closer look at these possibilities. First of all, we find that value systems can be as various as the individual community-members who live out these values. Clearly there must be some give and take among individuals and between communities. There must be some common basis of valuing if there is to be any cooperation and common product of their efforts. Yet pluralism is particularly evident here.

Among the members of a community of carpenters there will be quite different attitudes toward carpentry, unions, politics, family life, and God. Yet there must be enough sharing of common values so that six carpenters can build a solid house, so that one hundred fifty-three of them can form Local Twenty-Two of the Carpenters Union, so that they can pool their votes to elect a Democrat senator, so that the family men among carpenters can form families who occasionally like to get together for picnics and bowling. Still the value systems are different for each carpenter. After all, the uniqueness of the individual personality is very much the uniqueness of his scale of values as it rises and takes shape in the crucial decisions of his personal history.

Fortunately, however, within each man is an inner experience of himself which he likes to share with others: hope for children, the need to be recognized and loved, the need to return this love, sorrows over what might have been, laughter at the ridiculous and pompous, felt success or failure in work, loneliness, and a thousand other inner events whose common holding links man to man. In addition to this inner world, people share many external events with each other. This is their "outer world" of family meals, neighborhood scandals and gatherings, national wars, sporting events, the weather, depressions in business, and so on. All these outer experiences are given inner values which, along with the events, are almost unconsciously integrated into the individual personality—but as *commonly* shared and evaluated through conversation, verbal and nonverbal. Apparently the individual cannot form a value without its being shared in some way with another. For better or for worse, his life is simply not an isolated, telephone-booth existence unless he is psychotic. For this reason, no individual's value system is totally unsharable as though it were totally different from another's value system.

This common basis of evaluation leads naturally to the development of a communal system of values. The latter's accumulated history and strength must reciprocally influence the individual's value system from which the communal system originally arose. The almost sadistic attempt of some young people to distinguish their values from those of their parents only reveals how much of their parents' values they have previously accepted. The labor-union leader who successfully motivates his union membership to accept a particular labor contract is successful because he has found a basis on which to make his appeal. This basis is not merely the value system present in each individual but also the pressure generated by the group's collectively held values upon each individual in the group.

It is noteworthy, too, that this value system operative within the secularization process follows the lines of specialization and integration (socialization) which structure the process. For the value system is at once individually differentiated and socially integrated. Indeed, it rises fundamentally from a person's main life-skill, e.g., as student or housewife-mother or engineer or nurse or poet or lawyer or chemist—that skill to which the person devotes the major part of the day and by which he or she primarily describes the self.

Yet this skill or knowledge or technical expertise of the individual has little meaning and value except insofar as it works cooperatively within a particular skill-community for service of the larger communities. The TV repairman is helpless unless integrated within the television industry and entertainment world and unless serving their audience. Thus the individual value which the TV repairman gives to himself depends at least partially upon the communal value of his vocation to serve the television world. Nor can this value exceed realistically the degree of skill which the individual repairman possesses and the degree of good ideals, ideas, and techniques which the television world offers to mankind. The pride which the repairman takes in his skillful work and in his association with the television world is precisely his technical competence and his understanding of the television world insofar as he values the latter.

This same repairman also derives his personal value from his abilities to establish and maintain a good family life. His skill in budgeting family funds, in planning insurance security, in paying off mortgages, in disciplining the children, in assuring his wife that she is much more to him than a cook and a custodian of children, and so on, is a partial measure of his individual self-worth in family community. Further, his recreational skills of bridge-playing, bowling, fishing, telling stories, and just plain loafing with the family define his own self-value and his community-value. Secularization, or skillful dedication to the development of the world of persons, institutions, and things, is matched step-by-step by the individual's developing value system.

There is, however, a great single all-embracing value which simultaneously arises out of the individual and communal life-experiences of secularization and which embraces all the skills, knowledges, techniques, and consequent valuations of every individual and community.

This ultimate and total value is a person's world-view, his *Weltanschauung*.[14] Somehow man is man because he cannot long operate vitally without establishing for himself a value which is the total context of all other values and from which all other values get their vitality. This global value or total world evaluation may be the Marxist classless society, or the Sartrean acceptance of ultimate meaninglessness (irony of ironies), or the American secularist's perfectly democratic mankind, or the Buddhist's nirvana, or an individual's own self-aggrandizement, or his idealized family, or the Christian's union with the Trinity through the Body of Christ. This is Peter Berger's Sacred Canopy under which "all things make sense" and whose destruction in the windstorm of doubt and cynicism brings on the dark night of despair and of possible self-destruction, the total loss of meaning and value in life.

Of all values, this paramount one, for which alone man is ready to bleed to death, is most determinative. For it explains to man why, in the last resort, he should promote secularization or attack it or be indifferent to it. It is the final reason why man should love or hate the world, love or hate it more or less. Though often this all-encompassing value is operating deeply within man's experience, it surges into view dramatically when it is challenged by death or by success in some cherished enterprise.[15] Death of the TV repairman's wife or rapid expansion of his business can sharply determine his world-view and consequently change his evaluation of that secularization process of which his television world is a dynamic part.

In other words, the more clearly a man sees how his skills fit into and serve the various communities, that is, the more clearly he sees his place in the secularization process, then the more highly he can value his skills, his contributions, and himself. But the ultimate frame of reference for his vision and, therefore, for his valuing of the secularization process is his world-view. The godless man evaluates the world as a beautiful flux into which he pours his life so that his disappearance in death is the further building of that beauty. And the godly man who sees no continuation between the life-before-death and the life-after-death will estimate secularization quite differently from the godly man who sees this evolving world as a basis for the development of the world-after-death.

Would it be intemperate at this point to suggest that a positive value system is itself a dedication to the world, that it is a love eager to explore and to stretch out its arms to the whole of reality? This would be a secularity, a network of values (attitudes) structuring both the individual personality and the communal collective personality. The secularity would be working within and developing step-by-step with the secularization process. But then would one be merely the shadow of the other? Or are they really distinct factors, two different sides, of historical process?

Secularity, Reciprocal Effect and
Cause of Secularization

Are the values of the secularized man identical with his skills or knowledges or techniques so that the rationalization and routinization typical of secularization is precisely the valuing itself? Or is the valuing a response to the rationalization? Is the valuing a distinct effect of the rationalization and routinization—a distinct effect which rebounds back upon the rationalization and routinization of secularization in order to causally direct the latter's development?

If secularity is not distinct from secularization, then very likely secularity is not a freely developed system of values. Rather, it is either marching inevitably toward some single goal of Greek fate or it is stumbling blindly along toward some chance destination. On the other hand, if secularity is a factor really distinct from, yet always intimately involved in, secularization, then perhaps it is free enough to be born of secularization and yet to grow up to give mature direction to its parent's life—much like Athene, who learns to rule Zeus with intelligent love. This latter alternative would allow that secularization is progress. But it would also imply that the progress is no more inevitable or deterministic than man's ability to make free decisions according to freely accepted and freely developed values. Secularity, then, would be a freely accepted and directed dedication of man's heart (his value system) to the expansion of the world's beauty, personal and infrapersonal. It would pay us, therefore, to discover factually whether or not secularity is truly distinct, even though inseparable, from secularization. To this purpose, it would help to see how values arise within and promote secularization.

Because of the specialization of the scientific knowledges and skills, and because of man's capacity to integrate these knowledges and skills for the solution of a particular problem like pollution or transportation or increased power needs, man has attained a remarkable control over nature. Hydroelectric dams not only light his cities but also irrigate his orchards and make his wheat fields dense with yield. A rocket carries three men to the moon with millesecond precision. Because of improved communication systems and scientific procedures, government and business can organize their present work over millions of people and plan the future fifty years ahead. Man's masterful control over the world gives him a true sense of his autonomy and a feel for his dignity since he is building the universe with creative intelligence. No longer does he feel so weak and alone in the face of hostile natural elements. Now he experiences a new dimension of his freedom and a more compelling urge toward responsibility for the world and its future. Furthermore, for believers, God becomes less the God of lightning, floods, famines, and whirlwinds, and more the personal God who enters into covenants of friendship with His people.

Without the process of secularization, man could not exercise such power over the world and its people. Without this sense of power, he could not feel and thus value so deeply his own autonomy, freedom, responsibility for the world, and dignity before God. Evidently these values are caused by and consequent upon man's experience of the secularization process. Secularization self-fecundates and then gestates these values within herself.

But just as evidently these same values, though derived from the secularization experience, can in turn motivate man to devote his energies to further specialization of knowledges, skills, and techniques. The depth and location of this motivation will determine what particular sectors of the secularization process receive increased attention and how long this attention will perdure.[16] Such reciprocal causation by values on knowledges, skills, and techniques is put neatly by the phrase: "nothing breeds success like success." It is seen in the recent swift development of polio serum in medical technology to meet epidemics. The high value put on human life and the power to exercise the compassion of medicine for the sake of thousands of children were powerful stimulants for Drs. Salk and Sabin in their disciplined and sacrificial pursuit of the immunizing serum.

Of course, these values can be misused or at least misinterpreted so that they are employed by individuals against the secularization process. Here it is more clear that the values are really distinct from the process against which they are turned. For example, a psychologist could become so fascinated by the power of his specialized knowledge that he would try to make his patients dependent upon himself rather than to liberate them, that he would use his learning to divorce rather than to unite married couples, that he would come to contemn all other knowledges and skills in comparison with psychology. The value of his discipline, specialized out of philosophy and biology, would be used by him to disparage other knowledges and people rather than to integrate or socialize them. He would employ the effects of the secularization process, the consequent values, to motivate his attack on the process itself.

Other examples of this can be given. For instance, it is necessary continually to question all presuppositions in the sciences. But the value of this scientific procedure can be misapplied, e.g., to long-proven friendships, and can generate a paralyzing scepticism which, taken to its logical conclusion, would stop indirectly all contributions to the secularization process. A second example comes to mind. Out of the specialization of knowledges-skills-techniques and of their serving subcommunities has arisen a democratic system of checks and balances for the protection of liberty against oligarchy. But the resultant bureaucracy and its complex value system, which make secularization both possible and workable, can be turned against this process when the bureaucracy uses its values (e.g., efficiency, disposability of large public funds, ability to converge many experts on a specific problem) to corrupt and dominate citizens rather than to serve them. Still another example can be given of how values derived from secularization can be used to attack it. Man's sense of autonomy, given growth by his newly found control over nature, can be manipulated to deny the existence of God or man's need to worship Him. Strangely, the value of man's inner worth can be used to hide the value of God. Such a maneuver reduces the scope and effectiveness of secularization since it narrows unwarrantedly a plural approach to the world by leaving out the theistic and since it consequently undermines the theist's confidence in the secularization process.

With all these qualifications in mind, one can hazard a definition of secularity as a factor distinct from the secularization process yet contained within it—much as the influence of a football captain can arise out of, then permeate, next direct his teammates, yet be distinct from the latter. By this definition, then, secularity is a network of attitudes or values freely formed by men, individually and communally, in response to the secularization process and consequently employed at times to direct that same process toward the development of the universe.

Within the individual man and his community, secularity is the human factor seen more from its emotive and volitional side; while secularization would be the human factor seen more from its conceptual or rational side. There is no doubt that normally both sides work simultaneously and reciprocally. But equally sure is the insight that secularization is not secularity. For, to know something is not necessarily to value it. A more concrete definition of secularity is: that state which man has achieved through the development of specialized knowledges, skills, and techniques; namely, the state of sensing his own autonomy and freedom, his responsibility for the evolving universe, and his own dignity within a world-vision that does not necessarily exclude God.

This last codicil concerning the exclusion of God brings us to a large semantic difficulty. Not only is secularization often confused with secularity but also these two are frequently identified with a particular type of secularity called secularism. Therefore, in order to clear away this confusion, often enough promoted by secularistic campfollowers, consideration must be given to the various types of secularity present in the secularization process and particularly to one brand: atheistic secularism.

Secularism and Other Types of Secularity

Earlier it was noted how diverse were the value systems among individuals and between communities—so diverse that there was need to establish the common basis for these value systems or secularities. The diversity is due not merely to the diverse life-influences on individuals or communities but also to free decisions on their part. The most crucial of these free decisions is the calculated outlook of each man's world-view. For example, *humanistic secularity* will tend to make mankind the highest value in the universe and to declare artistic endeavor the supreme worship of man. *Pagan secularity* may well admit to the existence of some benevolent directing force within the universe which is called mother nature and may well consider the conservation of nature the highest act of love to this deity. *Christian secularity* discovers that the evolving universe is the created exteriorization of the

Trinitarian God's inner life, that Christ is a uniquely historical and universal man embodying all the potential of evolving mankind, and that mankind through Christ and His Church is meant to complete devoutly the Trinity's ongoing creation of the universe. Lastly, *secularism* finds that physical science is the only knowledge worthy of man, that the concept of God is a discarded hypothesis of physical science, and that man's sole path to nobility is the discovery and use of physical science for the better living or progress of mankind. These are only four out of many generic secularities, each of which has numerous species.[17]

But among these secularities, secularism must be given special attention because its proponents have often spoken as though secularism were the value-free secularization process itself. In achieving this confusion, the secularists have made it difficult for believers to cooperate with them. In hard fact, secularism in itself is a value system pretending to be pure science.[18] As a consequence of this pretense, it tends unwittingly to become a religion powered by a pharisaic zealotry.[19]

To understand these statements, one must notice how the roots of secularism are actually philosophic scientism. The basic tenet of scientism declares that the only true knowledge is physical science (social science will be acceptable only insofar as it is closely modeled on physical science). From this taproot and trunk of scientism branch all the values which constitute secularism. For, if the only way to knowledge is physical method, then all humanistic knowledge by way of the arts, literature, philosophy, and everyday experience, is simply shallow opinion. If this humanistic knowledge is the bridge between everyday living and faith-experience and yet is mere opinion, then faith is connected with the secularized world by a gossamer thread which, even if it exists, can hardly withstand the storms of life. On the basis of this prime tenet of scientism, therefore, secularism builds itself into a pure value system which devalues all knowledges other than physical science. Then, in supreme self-satisfaction with physical science, secularism first dogmatically insists that the universe is self-explanatory in simple physical terms, secondly decrees that God is unnecessary hypothetical baggage on life's journey, and thirdly announces grandly that man's nobility is to be built by science alone.

To propose secularism as more than a particular and somewhat arbitrary value system is to confuse it with scientism, which is its philosophic basis; or with secularity, of which it is only one instance in a class; or with secularization, which it inhibits more than it promotes.

Secularism is particularly harmful since it attacks the existence of mystery and myth.[20] Here, by mystery is meant that event or reality whose rich existence can be known by men but whose full meaning can be only partially and quite inadequately understood through the neat and maneuverable concepts of science or of philosophy. Mystery is much more murkily, yet also more completely, grasped by the imaginative language of literature and everyday experience. This latter expression is called myth. Both the mythic and the scientific approach are necessary to achieve a more adequate grasp of mystery; they supplement, clarify, and support each other. The love poetry of Donne is at least as important as the physiological studies of Masters and Johnson to the understanding of that mystery called married life, but must it not be supplemented by man's everyday experience of married love and by his faith-experience of what God asks of him in marriage?

The secularism of, e.g., Bertrand Russell, in its mistaken scientistic zeal, vastly underestimates the value of myth and thus tends to shrink the dimensions and warm beauty of mystery down to narrow, coldly abstract, scientific concepts. Further, it tends to disregard all other value systems and to limit man's view to its own bleak poverty. Here the democracy of a rich pluralism in value systems is reduced to the monistic zealotry of dictatorship.

Secularity, then, because it is concerned with value, is more in touch with myth and mystery than is the secularization process. For secularity goes beyond the conceptual and technical evidence of secularization and takes a stance toward the whole universe, human and divine, personal and infrapersonal. Any attempt to shrink secularity to mere secularism would not only impoverish twentieth-century man but jeopardize the whole secularization enterprise since the latter's growth depends on one's grasp of mystery through myth. For secularization, with its magnificent conceptual and technical apparatus, is forever exploring mystery, with the help of myth, in order to render mystery more intelligible and therefore more lovable. Secularization is not meant to supplant myth so much as to supplement it, to deny mystery so much as to clarify it. Perhaps at this point of rhetoric, it would be wise to check the validity of these distinctions among secularization, secularity, and secularism in the harsh light of current everyday problems.

SOME CIVIC PROBLEMS AND SECULARIZATION

Let us, therefore, focus these understandings of secularization process, secularity, and secularism upon some of our larger civic problems and watch to see whether or not fruitful insights are generated. Certain leading questions should be asked. For example, how is specialization and reciprocal integration (socialization) occurring in this particular problem? What type of secularity or value system would contribute better to the solution of this problem?

Clearly, only a very provisional and superficial interpretation of these problems is possible within the given limits of this article and its author. But perhaps the glimmering insights achieved may lure some social scientist into making a more profound study in order to check out the relevance of the previous philosophic analysis of secularization, secularity, and secularism.

Let us consider the problems of servant-class poverty, communication between subcommunities, "the establishment" and bigness, pluralism versus unity, racism, aesthetics amid rationalism, the ambivalence of technology, depersonalization and work, education's prolonging of adolescence, and alienation as a source of revolution. No attempt will be made to relate these problems except to indicate how each reveals the presence of the secularization process.

Servant-Class Poverty

To escape the poverty of the servant class, a person must acquire the skill and knowledge which make him valuable to a specialized subcommunity. If he is not a member of such a community (e.g., a union member, a doctor, a lawyer, a physicist, a policeman, a social worker), he floats alone like a mote caught by fitful air-drafts and he is at the mercy of the organized subcommunities. He does not serve a particular master so much as a master-community. For example, nurses' aides in hospitals and nursing homes were regularly underpaid until unionized. Now, to acquire the skill or knowledge necessary for escaping the poor servant class, one must be educated. Yet education is rapidly becoming more and more expensive, not merely in money but especially in time, and therefore threatens to become less open to the poor. For the specialization of knowledges and skills is accelerating to the degree that even those already skilled have to take refresher courses. Thus, unless proper steps are taken, the distance between the unskilled and the skilled person may increase rather than decrease, since the poor must work while simultaneously seeking education. Specialization, when accelerated without simultaneous acceleration of integration between classes, could fragment society.

This raises the questions: What can be done to give the poor more time for education? What can be done to alert them to their deepening need for continuing education? What type of secularity best conveys the dignity of the poor so that its values can lure us into the intricate labor of accelerating societal integration?

Communication Between Subcommunities

The more specialized knowledges and skills become, then the more specialized become their serving communities and the more there is required increased knowledge and skill for communication between these serving communities. Where once most of the major philosophers (Leibniz, Kant, Descartes, etc.) were also top-flight physicists and mathematicians, this rarely happens nowadays. Indeed, the communication between philosophy and physics through, for example, philosophy of science is perilous even to the experts.[21] On the more practical level, the problems of the bus drivers' union are difficult to describe to the banker who limousines to work.

Admittedly, the secularization process, in developing subcommunities which individually counterbalance each other and which collectively stand up against big government, big business, big crime, has developed the possibilities of freedom for modern man.[22] This is beneficial socialization. However, the diminishment of communication-ability consequent upon intense specialization also offers more opportunities for conflict because of belligerent prejudice and warring special interests. For this reason, a special effort must be made to bridge the gaps, to provide socialization. Some possible means of increasing societal integration could be reemphasis of liberal education, establishment of arbitration boards made up of representatives from various specialized communities, and motivations (secularity) stressing the brotherhood of all men. In this last instance, it would seem that something more than secularism's brotherhood-by-genetics is needed.

The "Establishment" and Bigness

Specialization demands bigness. For example, in the business world, specialization requires large sums of money to do research, to package, to market, to advertise, to finance over long periods. Further, no company can long live on one product; it must diversify to survive. Indeed, it must combine with other companies so that weakness is paired off against strength for tax write-offs, for the sharing of common merchandising structures, and for the equalizing of risk-ventures in new products. Bigness is a form of socialization (integration) brought on by specialization. In other words, only bigness can handle the growing complexity and the spiraling expenses brought on by specialization and socialization. The bigness, of course, can be the occasion for the mechanized merchandising of the personal in faceless and seemingly unscrupulous procedures such as the sudden layoff at the mills, inadequate pension funding, or assembly-line speedups. But no small part of these frustrations have been reduced by recent socialized cooperation between management and the labor forces.

What is said of big business is just as true of big government for many of the same reasons; just as true of big university, just as true of big crime and big law enforcement. All these form that interlocking directorate called "the establishment" against which the have-nots protest. However, despite all the protests, bigness is here to stay so long as secularization is here to stay. And the latter will be operative so long as large populations must be fed, clothed, housed, and entertained. For only the specialization and super-organization (socialization) of secularization makes the support of large populations possible. A short strike by the transport workers of America would prove this point quickly, yet they form only one cog in the great industrial machine.

One response of big business, big government, and big university to the problem of bigness has been to use the subsidiarity principle: local decisions must be made by local authority according to the widely diverse local conditions (specialization). Yet all the local organizations and their decisions must be unified nationally (socialization) through the use of computerized criteria of success and failure, through instant reports of decisions by private communications systems, through lobbying combines at state and national legislatures, and through cooperative use of the parent company's subsidiary units (e.g., the canning subsidiary uses its sister trucking subsidiary). This is called democratization of the decision process and socialization of business procedures.

But ultimately, as bigness becomes more and more powerful, the temptation of individuals and of groups to abuse power must be balanced by a new secularity. The latter would underline each person's duty to protect the weak and to build into bigness more and more procedures which allow for the liberty, inventiveness, and growth of the small.

Pluralism versus Unity

Pluralism among faiths, political parties, philosophies of life, societies, etc., is a direct result of secularization. For the specialization among knowledges and skills and among their serving communities is matched by other types of specialization occurring within each knowledge- or skill-community. For this latter community is composed of people from diverse faiths, educational philosophies, nationalities, ambitions, and ways of life. But their unity is achieved through common devotion to a common skill or knowledge *for very different reasons.*[23] Thus, within the same subcommunity, the ultimate plausibility structure by which a man lives sanely may be suddenly challenged by the contrasting final plausibility structure of a fiancée or of colleagues on a particular job.[24] As a result of the secularization process, one cannot avoid confrontations of ultimate value-systems or secularities.[25] Here compromise is not always a sacrifice of one's commitment to a value; it may well be an insight into a previously unseen basis for agreement—an insight generated by the confrontation of ultimate value systems. This is the ambivalence of the phenomenon of secularity: at times the clash of various value-systems brings on the debilitating fever of ambivalence and conflict; on other occasions it produces a new vigor of thought and a deeper community of action.

Racism

Specialization in forming communities according to skills and knowledges could well lead to the breakdown of overly severe divisions between communities based on blood or religious ties. This would be the socialization element of secularization. But at the same time, secularization can offer the opportunity for men to accentuate racial divisions if a particular race generally lacks the skills and knowledges necessary to become members of these skill- and knowledge-communities. Once a race is generally placed by prejudice in a servant class which can hardly acquire the skills necessary for upward mobility in society, then even those members of the race who attempt with capability to move upward are held back frustratingly by societal mores. Thus there may come a time when the only resort left seems to be South American rioting or South African enclaves—both self-destroying options.

Here again, the secularities which contain strong compassion for the downtrodden—a compassion which reaches out beyond national barriers and class distinctions—can lead men to invent new ways to heal the divisions consequent on specialization. These ways may be as widely diverse as state scholarships, on-job training of the unskilled, school busing, organization of the Third World labor-forces by Western unionizers, world government, and ecumenism.

Aesthetics amid Rationalism

Secularization is characterized by rationalization; that is, by highly abstract conceptualizations used as tools for understanding the complexity of the real situation. This

is true even of the social sciences, for example, psychometrics, sociological statistical data, the constructs of economics (gross national product, living wage index, and
so on). Such abstractions, powerful instruments that they
are, nevertheless need the balance of other knowledges in
a man so that he does not lose his sense of life's wholeness
and mystery—that reality which is touched, even explored,
by conceptualization but which is never exhausted by it.

Even common sense knowledge of everyday life is
not enough to supply man's need for the concrete emotive
grasp of life's wholeness. Thus the more urbanized, the
more rationalized, and the more secularized our civilization becomes, the more needed will be one's grasp of the
concrete, emotive, imaginative whole of life. This need is
filled by art, music, drama-poetry, sculpture, landscape,
and sports. For these skills and arts are the universal,
heightened, and stylized expression of man's common
everyday experience of the concrete whole situation. They
are needed to help him appreciate and live the whole of
everyday life. Thus the more recent emphasis on the artistic in American life (even to the do-it-yourself kits and
to the filling in of numbered squares for amateur paint-
ing) reveals a growing sense of fragmentation and a consequent desire to experience wholeness.

Nevertheless, the more massive the need for art because of secularization's specialization or rationalization,
the greater the danger of philistinism (commercialized or
purely financial or technocratic art) and the greater the
danger of cheap art (no small part of the television and
publishing industries) and of sheer emotionalism (e.g.,
theater of confrontation)—all of which, ironically, further
fragment man's consciousness.

Indeed, unless the piecemeal specialization of rational analysis is balanced by a heightened sense of the integrating-socializing wholeness of everyday experience, man tends to lose the total meaning of his work in detailed analysis, tends to lose sight of the universe and its historic sweep in a blizzard of nonessentials, tends to forget the most perduring and fulfilling values of those mysterious wholes called person, family, community, hope in the future, and faith in a provident God.

Here it becomes clear that any secularity which excludes one or another of these values when they are producing wholesomeness would debilitate the secularization process. Consequently, the secularity called secularism, insofar as it denies the relevance of God to the universe and attempts to reduce man's scientific consciousness to the physical sciences, not only impoverishes but even gravely endangers the secularization process. For secularism tends to deny the wholeness of man's experience of the world, of God, and of himself.

The Ambivalence of Technology

The technology operative in mass production, computerized business operations, automation, and mass communications is not merely the result of secularization, but is also a reciprocal cause of it. Not only has science given us the steam and gas engines as well as electrical circuitry, but the latter have made possible the computer system which in turn makes possible the study of genetics, of star dust, of sociological data, of psychometrics, and of scriptural and patristic parallel texts.

Technology promotes with its tools not only the specialization of sciences into further and further subdivisions but also the specialization of skills built around particular machines (electron microscopes, laser beam cutters, punch presses, typewriters, filing machines, etc.). Technology also has a socializing effect. For example, a medical team performing a kidney operation, open-heart surgery, a transplant, or postnatal care for premature infants must work and suffer together as a community united through complex machinery for the preservation and increase of life. In this way technology not only frees men from the limitations of time, space, and poverty, but also forms community. However, this same socialization in teamwork can also be used for enslaving other men through the brain-washing of communication systems, through the diplomatic blackmail of atomic rocketry, and through the economic rigging of international trade.

Evidently, the secularization process taken philosophically remains neutral until man begins to use it for good or evil according to a particular secularity.

Depersonalization and Work

The more specialized a person's job or role in life becomes, the more susceptible he is to fragmentation. Further, the more susceptible the individual person is to fragmentation, the less able he is to relate to others and the more atomized becomes his community, since the fragmentation isolates individuals from their family, their neighborhood, and their nation.

The reason for this direct connection between role-specialization and personality-fragmentation is that such specialization makes more difficult a personal synthesis or life-integration. A person has so many diverse roles to integrate within his single person. For example, a man must be not only father, husband, and supermarket manager, but also clever financial expert, parish catechist, household repair man, and Boy Scout leader. On the other hand, the woman may be not only the daughter nursing her rapidly aging mother and the widow raising three teen-age boys, but also the fashion merchandiser who must be skillful in advertising, selling, and tailoring and who incidentally helps out the local political party precinct captain. How can this man or this woman fit together all these roles so that a "meaningful wholesome life" results?

Further, each man and woman has to find his or her particular role in this fast-moving, ever-twisting world of ours. But the more complicated the civilization in which we live, the more difficult it is for us to achieve the synthesis or overview necessary to find one's proper role and to value it. Not only are many greatly diverse overviews offered a person (e.g., Marxism, Christianity, secularism, evolutionary relativism, anarchism) to confuse as well as to enrich him; but also the evidence for any one view in all its complexity is harder and harder to assess for its truthfulness.

As a result, he can give up on all overviews, or he can attempt to straddle two overviews (with all the consequent frustration and agony), or he can arbitrarily choose one overview instead of others and form himself into a zealot, or he can patiently work out his overview through many years of experience. But in any one of the four options, he risks losing the meaning of his job-skill-knowledge by losing the meaning of life's overview. For the meaning of one's work is at the center of one's overview and receives vibrant life from it. Here socialization, because of its increased complexity, seems to make specialization less possible.[26] Thus, without a benevolent secularity, the health of the secularization process is in danger.

Further, when meaning begins to drain out of one's

job or role in life, one feels depersonalized, i.e., less valuable and less useful. Then a person's work-activity becomes futile arm waving, futile running on a coolie's endless wheel-pump, futile shouting in the great cavern of the huge factory or office. At this point the worker does not expect or hope for positive evaluation from his wife, children, friends—except for qualities which really are not central to his life, for example, champion at the local bowling palace, the great vacationer, the magnificent womanizer, the best-dressed man on the block, the fastest driver in the state, the guy whose kids go to the ritziest school, the man who knows the President's first cousin. Man's inner worth is to be measured mainly by exterior ornaments. Under these conditions specialization and socialization seem to inhibit each other and to cause fragmentation of the human person in whom they operate, unless a beneficial secularity helps to knit the fragments together.

Education's Prolonging of Adolescence

The specialization involved in secularization makes seemingly contradictory demands on the young person. It tells him to concentrate narrowly and intensely on acquiring a very complex skill or knowledge. Yet socialization, the ability to influence and to be influenced by other skills, knowledges and subcommunities, requires a broad-based knowledge and sympathy for other skills, knowledges, and communities. Is this a prescription for the old liberal arts curriculum without much specialization?

Specialization, in demanding early commitment to a special skill or knowledge and in requiring an ever more prolonged education, seems to make the socialization of marriage and of civic dedication more and more remote as the adolescent's dependence on full parental economic support extends far into his twenties. What is worse, the leisured affluence of American society tends to make suffering less and less bearable even if it cannot remove all suffering. At the same time the restless mobility of business life, transportation, ideas, and entertainment tends to undermine long-term commitment. Thus the three important stimulants to maturity and responsibility: marriage, suffering, commitment to community, are less powerful. In these ways, specialization seems to be the occasion of a weakening of socialization. How enjoy both specialization and socialization without sacrificing one or the other? For, without specialized skills and knowledges our civilization will grind to a paralyzed halt; without socialization, it will explode into violent fragments.

In starting out on the long education trek, American young people are endeavoring to catch up to their parents, their neighborhood, their city and nation. But each five years, the youngsters have to run harder and longer. For the skills, knowledges, and subcommunities must become ever more complex in order to master the growing problems presented them by cumulative social change in the larger community. Because of the suffering and tensions involved in the great chase, the youngsters begin to ask whether it is all worthwhile; they challenge the unquestioned suppositions upon which the previous generation built its pursuit of the good life. The ironic contradiction is that the answer to these questions must come at least partially from the experience of mastery in the developing use of these skills and knowledges and in the shaping of one's subcommunity according to socialization. And yet this experience is precisely what the student has not yet attained and what he cannot attain except by way of the education process whose worth he is doubting. In a sense, he feels that he has to challenge and question this society before he is fully integrated into it and before he can experience it. Otherwise he is already trapped in it. He is tempted to deny the worth of that which he cannot know well enough to deny.

In the midst of this educational anomaly, he is being asked not merely to play the role of student but to give total dedication to it so that his spontaneity (which he often confuses with freedom) is greatly restricted. He is asked to make a gigantic act of divine confidence in the ruling generation (of the falsified expense account, of three wars, of petty morality); he is asked to become mature when the values needed for maturity (family, suffering, commitment) are deteriorating. This ambivalence is further intensified as the student begins to realize that if he survives the long educational journey, at least three other treks just as difficult are offered him. He must climb the mountain of mercantile advancement or political power or ecclesiastical preferment. The establishment not only controls his education but also claims to be the prize for which, like Hercules, he must perform "just one more (seemingly impossible) feat."

At this point in his life, the student must discover a secularity ("an honest one," as he says) which will enable him to make the basic choice: either to join society and better it or to abandon society and let it get worse. In no case can he avoid using a secularity, and the one he chooses will determine how he lives—within or out of secularization: to promote it or to attack it.

A Source of Revolution: Alienation

Is it any wonder, then, that some youths give up on the "specialization bit" and attempt to return through time to a supposedly golden age of simple life and instant community based on spontaneous affection? Since socialization seems to be put off for so long or since only its pressuring of youth into the specifications of society is observed, some youths impatiently rebel—even though the shrewd ones know implicitly that the destruction of specialization would mean starvation and indescribable physical and mental misery. Because of this ambivalence, they feel forced to stress honesty, integrity, commitment, communal experience, personalism—all the qualities which they feel are lacking most in the previous generation and in themselves. Their long educational servitude, as they see it, has robbed them of the opportunities for discovering their own personal identity, has increased their juvenile dependence on adults, and is impossible to change without destroying the whole establishment.

Because of his frustration with the establishment, the student often enough feels the need to epitomize it as "impersonalism itself" and then to stress personalism against socialization in a very individualistic sense ("I've got to do my thing even if people don't like it, even if it hurts a lot of people"). No higher value seems to exist unless it be the co-value called "primacy of experience." Once all presuppositions of one's culture are found questionable, once confidence in the previous generation's report of their experience is lost, then one is left with only one's own individual direct experience of reality, limited as this experience may be. Not just commonsense knowledge becomes the highest value, rather the individual's personal commonsense knowledge is made the ultimate and really sole criterion for decision. All scientific knowledge is explicitly rejected and implicitly used. Again, confusion and hypocrisy. For all specialization of knowledges is rejected on principle. Consequently, much of modern civilization must be renounced on principle—although, to survive, the renouncer must live off this civilization like some virus.

This individualism, with its drive to instant spontaneous community, is paradoxically also a rejection of socialization. It is an attempt to set up primitive community in the midst of civilized community when the former must, like a parasite, live off the latter or destroy it in order to survive. The so-called democracy of this primitive community is basically anarchist in its extreme individualism. Only insofar as it imitates the rejected community by setting up a division of labor and then a system of balances and checks on authority does this community become democratic and avoid the rigid authoritarianism of primitive community. But then such a community begins to resemble more and more the very community it has rejected.

All these frustrations lead to the violent revolutions of the disturbed personality, the personality which is suffering the bitter frustration of seemingly inescapable internal contradiction. The difference, however, is that the personality here is a collective one. It screams slogans, projects its self-hate on society in wall-scribbling, attacks the innocent as well as the guilty, lives in squalor as a sign of its despair, is tempted to destroy while pleading innocence and the highest ideals, eloquently describes a world-view which takes for granted the eventual abolition of sin, work, suffering, disappointment, and deceit. In rejecting the specialization of secularization, this alienated community must reject the socialization attendant on secularization.

It must destroy modern civilization or be destroyed. Therefore it must turn to totalitarian techniques because modern civilization is so powerful a foe; it must use the basic organs of modern civilization to destroy her. Ironically, the university as the principal agent of secularization must be first and foremost the instrument for destroying the modern Western civilization which it has built. The university must furnish the techniques of subversion, the communications media for propaganda, the professorial support for violence, and above all, the great myth (communism, anarchism, secularism) by which the revolutionary fires will be lit, stoked, and spread to burn, gut, and level modern civilization so that on its ashes a new society free from evil may be built. Of course, the very growth of this society will occur by ways of specialization and consequent socialization, and its success in creating good over evil will be commensurate with the adequacy of its dominant secularity to meet its developing needs and problems.

SOME CONCLUSIONS

Perhaps we are now ready to venture some conclusions, not so much because they are thought to derive inevitably from the previously advanced ideas but more because they may serve to stimulate further investigations into secularization and secularity as factors for measuring progress and regress.

(1) Secularization, taken in itself or philosophically, seems to be a neutral process, which, through reciprocal specialization and integration of knowledges, skills, and procedures, builds the individual human personality and the collective communal personality out of cumulative interaction. In this sense, secularization can be only progress.

(2) But secularity, taken as the attitudinal value-

response to secularization and as the later directive force within secularization, is not neutral. Because it includes many diverse value-systems, it has degrees of goodness ranging from atheistic secularism to Christian secularity. Insofar as a particular secularity is unrealistic or inadequate to a situation, it encourages evil and hampers the secularization process. For secularity, being a dedication to the world, directs secularization and fashions it histori cally for good or evil, for progress or regress, according to the historical value-decisions of definite men and communities. Thus secularization taken historically is never neutral, since it is always being directed from within by various collaborating and conflicting secularities whose overall collective thrust determines the progress or regress of the secularization process taken historically.

(3) Secularization taken historically appears to be a controlled revolution or a healthy evolution of man and of world when it is directed by a dominant secularity which is adequate to the situation. But an inadequate or less realistic secularity, if dominant, could induce regression into the secularization process. For specialization, unrelieved by a matching integration or socialization, can be directed to atomize man and his world if the dominant secularity is individualistic. Or socialization can be used to stifle the initiative and inventiveness necessary for specialization if a particular directing secularity values short-term collective efficiency over individual liberty. In either case individual and communal secularization are mutually weakened. This decline of civilization, and hence of culture, would head for barbarism and violence as the world population begins to starve physically, psychologically, and spiritually.

(4) Philosophic secularization, because of its neutral openness to either progress or regress under the driving force of various secularities, will have its future directed by man's free choice among competing value-systems or secularities. These historical choices render secularization no longer neutral but historically committed for good and for evil. Thus secularization, taken historically, is both good and bad, never all good nor all bad, never totally progressive nor totally regressive. Thus, too, secularization, taken historically, has many faces, many definitions; economic, artistic, psychological, sociological, theological, and so on. But lying underneath all these phenomena of secularization and giving them energy is secularization taken philosophically, an unending cumulative process of reciprocal specialization within and socialization among various knowledges, skills, and their serving communities.

(5) A quick survey of some contemporary societal problems suggests:

   a that secularization is quite distinct from secularity and, therefore, from that particular secularity called secularism;

   b that one must choose carefully among various competing secularities lest the secularization process be hindered by an inadequate secularity;

   c that secularism is one of the less adequate secularities.

(6) Thus the progress of man is occurring according to his secularization taken philosophically. But the crisis of man is his wavering between various competing secularities and his growing impatience with that complexity of secularization which is necessary for the responsible development of man and of his world.

(7) If progress is simply a growing secularization taken philosophically, then the deepening of specialization is a measure of progress *if* it is accompanied by a balancing growth of socialization (integration) on the part of both the individual and the community. This gives us four parameters for measuring progress: specialization and socialization, both individual and communal. To this may be added a fifth parameter: the adequacy with which the predominant secularity promotes the secularization process.

chapter III

Frank J. Yartz, Ph.D.

Progress and the Crisis of Man

Prior to 1900 the great evolutionary hypotheses of such thinkers as Darwin and Spencer gave to the world the hope that some day the cosmos would reach its highest level of perfection. The hypotheses stressed that the disappearance of degenerate elements in nature would give rise to a superior reality. In fact the optimistic strain of Spencer's thought stressed that this would come about as a matter of necessity, not merely by accident. Spencer says:

> What we call evil and immorality must disappear. It is certain that man must become perfect.[1]

The hope of Marxism itself—an offshoot of evolutionary thinking—is that through science man can and will achieve his Utopia.

As the years of the early part of the twentieth century elapsed, the optimism of the evolutionists was dampened in certain parts of the world. The attitude of certain progressiveness was changed to a hope of nonretrogression. W. R. Inge writes in the year 1920:

We must cut down our hope for our nation, for
Europe, for humanity at large, to a very modest and
humble aspiration. We have no millennium to
look forward to, but neither need we fear any
protracted or widespread retrogression. There will
be new types of achievement which will enrich
the experience of the race. . . . They will not
merely repeat the triumphs of the past, but will
add new variety to the achievements of
the human mind.[2]

Inge has neither good nor bad news regarding the
progress of man. He is of course not as optimistic as the
evolutionists mentioned, but he does not espouse as de-
pressing a view as that of John Morley in *Educational
Review*. Morley writes:

To think of progress as a certainty is superstitious
—the most splendid of all superstition still. It
is a kind of fatalism—radiant, confident, and
infinitely hopeful—yet fatalism still, and like
fatalism in all its other forms, inevitably dangerous
to the effective sense of individual responsibility.[3]

If one looks around today in the latter part of the
twentieth century, one might not be so apt to look upon
the progress of man with the scepticism of the earlier
decades. In fact one might claim progress is buzzing all
over. It is possible for a traveler to have breakfast in New
York, lunch in Chicago, and be home in San Francisco
the same evening for dinner. The miracles of television
have made every person living in a civilized and free
country almost instantly informed of current events, re-
gardless of how far away they take place. And to make

the story of progress sound even more successful, not so long ago we viewed on the television screen that "giant step" of mankind, the landing on the surface of the moon. No doubt these are outstanding instances of progress that persons who lived in the beginning of the century might never have imagined as possible.

We are a progress-conscious people. We hear persons speaking of progress all over. General Electric makes millions of dollars selling electrical equipment, but advertises that its "most important product is progress." *Business Week* printed an advertisement by Container Corporation of America, in which the philosopher A. N. Whitehead was quoted: "The act of progress is to preserve order amid change, and to preserve change amid order."[4] The company apparently boasts of trying to keep in line with Whitehead's philosophical observation.

The *New Yorker* reminds us of further progress-consciousness of our time in an article on the World's Fair that was held in Osaka, Japan, in 1970.[5] The theme of the fair was "Progress and Harmony of Mankind." The fair itself stressed progress of the computer age. It showed: how one could get an appraisal of one's taste in clothes by selecting the components of an imaginary outfit and having a computer comment on its harmoniousness. The fair also gave Osaka, Japan, an opportunity to boast of its three-hundred-ten-mile railroad that operates at very high speeds and through a computer refunds passenger fares if the trains are unwarrantedly delayed. But the *New Yorker* emphasized that Japan has no diplomatic relations with Red China even though Japan sells much of its merchandise to that nation. Thus, while there may be progress in the world, there is not harmony among mankind.

Around the meaning of the theme of the fair—
"Progress and Harmony for Mankind"—revolves a series
of questions which lie at the heart of a philosophy of
progress. Does the theme mean scientific progress and
social harmony? Does it mean social harmony through
scientific progress? Or, social progress through social harmony? An attempt at answering these questions brings
us to a discussion of the crucial problem of progress.
Despite the fact that we can point to much scientific
advancement, we are also faced with numerous examples
of disharmony among men. These indeed make us wonder
whether man has ever really advanced from the level of
the tooth-and-claw age of the caveman. At the present time
wars continue to rage and to cost many lives. Our cities
are being plundered by social unrest caused by our failure
to reckon with the problem of social injustice of the past.
We seem to be in a state of change—maybe chaos, maybe
revolution. Many have tried to explain what is going on;
but rather than give answers, they end with the question,
Are we making progress?

Thus, there is ample evidence of our progress-
consciousness of recent times. Moreover, within the scope
of our zeal to be progressive people, the philosophical
problems of progress appear—especially, the fact that scientific progress does not easily translate into social harmony.

An attempt will be made to open up the meaning of
"progress." First, we will see the word "progress" unfold
to mean change. Second, we will show it to unfold further
to include novelty. At various times in history it has been
difficult to discern this constituent.

Third, the relationship among the individual, society, and progress will be discussed. Not all philosophers agree as to the importance of the individual in the story of man's progress. Some stress the individual at the expense of cutting man out of the social context and vice versa. The golden middle must be found. It is as false to say man is society as it is to say society means each individual acting only for himself.

The question of the priority of social progress over scientific progress and vice versa emerges as important. If scientific progress is overstressed, man becomes a scientific object. This can dehumanize the individual person. But to ignore scientific progress means to deny a crucial factor in the story of man's progress. Science can be used to aid relations among persons. A discussion of progress, then, must end up in a discussion of the meaning of man in his relations to the world. One can only hope to achieve the meaning of progress in the scope of a relational context.

PROGRESS AND CHANGE

If all things were at a standstill, there would be no hope for a bad situation to improve. Things must move on for advancement to be realized. But only certain changes are progressive. While it is correct to claim change is necessary for progress, it is false to conclude all change is progressive. Important distinctions must be made. (1) Change with no direction to it is not progressive. It is confused, and goes nowhere. (2) Change which moves backward is regressive, rather than progressive. (3) Progressive change moving in the forward direction is change for the better. G. K. Chesterton is strong in his view that progress involves direction:

> For progress by its very name indicates direction
> and the moment we are in the least doubtful about
> direction, we become in the same degree
> doubtful about progress.[6]

Let us carry the argument a step further. While it is reasonable to conclude that progress is change which admits of direction for the better, whatever the good may be in the specific instance involved, the question still remains: What determines this directedness? On viewing the motions of the legislature as it tries to put a bill through Congress one can ask, What determines the direction that the action of the legislature takes? The answer is a goal, and only the person with a goal in mind can assess the progressiveness of any action. Moreover, the notion of goal implies value. An early twentieth-century sociologist brings out the importance of value to the notion of progress:

> Progress is not synonymous with change, for
> change may be for better or worse, it means mere
> quantitative variation and implies no idea of
> value . . . progress is evolution measured by
> an assumed standard of human value.[7]

The notion of progress not only involves a metaphysics of goals, but also an ethics of norms, for goals are normative. A philosophy that does not admit of goal-directedness cannot admit of progress. An ethics that is not normative is not in reality a progressive ethics. To a philosopher who claims ethics is just a description of the behavior of a certain group of persons in a certain time and social culture, progress is a meaningless word—at least in any unambivalent sense of the term. To the evolutionists who think that nature follows certain laws, has a definite pattern of activity, and is teleologically oriented, "progress" means much. That is the reason the evolutionists—whether Spencer or Darwin or even Chardin—discuss the topic of progress at great length. To an epistemology that does not have any place for objectivity, progress becomes a confused notion. For if progress is only a subjective notion, radically conflicting views can all be said to be progressive at the same time, in which case the relativism that results reduces progress to a meaningless notion.

Leonard Krieger, who undertook a study of the meaning of the contemporary notion of progress, is correct in his claims that the concept of progress "is a composite of two elements—it is both a summary of judgments on the quality of human experience and a component of ideals for the molding of that experience," and also that in the twentieth century "the results of sociological and historical investigations of social reality have undermined the absolute validity of ideals. Epistemology has tended to undermine the meaningfulness of the objective world"[8] The anthropologist Stanley Casson in his book *Progress and Catastrophe* poetically describes progress as that which "implies not merely movement onward from one point to another . . . but a movement in the course of which something is picked up *en route* which transforms the progress into a triumphal procession."[9] This is a far cry from what Krieger must conclude is an acceptable view today.

The notion of progress is, in the final analysis, something very close to all of us in our day-to-day lives. Let us not talk on a philosophical plane, but merely on the practical day-to-day level. If persons thought that progress was something totally unattainable in any activity, claiming life was absurd, they would have no reason for wanting to carry on their lives. Someone who suffered a serious financial setback would not be able to look forward to better times. Someone who becomes ill needs to realize the possibility of progress for him to continue in such a way that he will get better. The notion of progress is essential to the meaning of life. Of course, the question arises, Is one fooling oneself in thinking progressively? Well, sometimes maybe, but if that were the case always, one would have to give up. Surely, in a world where the H-bomb or the radiation from it could destroy all of civilization, one begins to wonder about progress in this life or maybe even to think about the possibility of progress with relation to the afterlife. At any rate, for a philosopher to tell the layman that life cannot admit of progress in any manner at all would be more of a death blow to the philosopher and his philosophy than to progress-theory itself. It is insanity to press regression too far.

PROGRESS AND NOVELTY

So far the relationship among progress, action, and goal-direction has been mentioned. It is true enough that progress involves all these elements, but this is not the entire story. Action can be cyclical in nature and yet be goal-directed. In the long run this kind of action is not to be called progressive. Progress involves breaking the cycle with novelty.

The notion of novelty could involve revolution in a political, scientific, or any of several other senses. Revolution basically means irresistibility to the past—that is, change that takes place (social, political, etc.) becomes too strong to allow the old established order to prevail. But revolution has not always meant that. Hannah Arendt[10] tells us of the history of the word. Originally it was a scientific term referring to the revolving motion of the stars. This sense of the word is found in Copernicus's *De revolutionibus orbium coelestium*, and it does not connote newness or violence. It does, however, refer to a cyclical motion beyond the control of men and, hence, irresistible.

The word "revolution" even as meaning cyclical motion can be taken out of the scientific context and applied to the human situation on earth to mean an irresistible domination of successes and failures. Just as the sun and moon and stars come out each day, so too man is irresistibly bound up with woes. Woes come and go in a cyclical fashion; woes involve going back to some pre-established order.

It was not until the night of July 14, 1789, that the word "revolution" was used for the first time to mean irresistibility outside of the context of cyclical motion. On that day King Louis XVI learned of the fall of the Bastille from Duc de La Rochefoucauld-Liancourt. The king responded, "C'est une révolte." Liancourt corrected him by saying, "Non, Sire, c'est une révolution."[11]

The history of the word "revolution" indicates clearly enough that in the spirit of the ancient Greek notion of change as cyclical, revolution as change had to be cyclical also. The word has evolved in meaning from the sense of revolution of the planets, to the sense of man's destiny revolving back under the direction of the planets, then to a political usage in which finally the cycle of revolution (or turning around in a circle) was broken. To say revolution means breaking the cycle is the equivalent of saying it means dealing with the future, not the past, and hence with progress rather than regression. Revolutions, however, may backfire and lead to regression, if the original goals are not authentic or if authentic goals are not realized.

There exists a twilight zone between change of certain types and revolutionary activity. Crane Brinton, when he analyzes various revolutions—English, French, Russian, and American—claims that only the extreme cases of revolution are easy to point out.

> We do not entangle ourselves unduly with the exact definition of revolution, nor with the borderline between revolutionary change and other kinds of change. . . . The difference between a revolution and other kinds of change in societies is, to judge from many past users of the term, logically nearer to that between a mountain and a hill than to that, say, between the freezing point and the boiling point of a given substance. The physicist can measure boiling points exactly.[12]

It may be difficult to pinpoint the difference between that type of change going on today and revolutionary action. For the present let us just make a listing of what Brinton calls symptoms of revolution:

(1) Society on the upgrade economically.

(2) Bitter class antagonism.

(3) Transfer of allegiance of the intellectuals.

(4) Government machinery inefficient because of a failure to make changes in old institutions. New conditions lay an intolerable strain on government machinery.

(5) Old ruling class loses faith in itself.[13]

(Of course, it must be kept in mind that in those borderline cases between revolution and swift change, these symptoms can be strongly disputed.)

To summarize, we might say that progress involves change for the better. The notion of "better" involves goal-direction. Change must look to the future, for cyclical change is not really progressive—it looks to the past. As the cycle of action breaks, newness can come about through revolution. But not all novelty is revolution. Moreover, it is at times impossible to distinguish between those nonextreme cases. So the distinction between revolution and novelty must remain at times unclear.

PROGRESS AND SOCIAL RELATIONS

Let us open up a new perspective on the meaning of progress—that of social relations. To an important extent our discussion of revolution is related to the meaning of progress through social relations. But it is important to note that revolution is the means to progress. It is not an end in itself. Those who revolt do so for the purpose of achieving some end. Revolution for the sake of revolution is not progressive action; rather it is a nonprogressive, chaotic activity.

Even though revolution may in some instances be necessary for progressiveness, social progress is nonetheless characterized by harmony among men. How is this harmony attained? The answer is: In action that is in accord with common goals. Common goals, a basis for understanding and communicating among men, enable a group of people to make headway. However, one can stress too heavily the notion of unity among individuals. Too much unification can lead to inaction. In other words, if everybody always agrees with everybody else, the world could come to a standstill. Difference is essential to social progress, but not the kind of difference—radical difference—that stifles unity of aims. That type of difference is as nonprogressive as the type of unity that hinders activity.

Thus unity-in-difference is needed for social progress. Another word for unity-in-difference is relationship. The *ratio* or central meaning of social progress is relations among men. No man can advance by cutting himself off from the rest of society. We need each other for our own fulfillment. An individual progresses only insofar as he relates to others.

Not to relate to the world is not even psychically healthy. How does a psychiatrist get his patient back to normalcy? By getting the patient to learn again how to relate to the world. Relation of the individual person to the world aids the person as well as society.

Now, relation involves more than goal-directedness. It is possible for an individual to direct his life in line with certain goals, but still be unable to avoid conflicts with the goals that others have established. Through relation, however, the problem of conflict of goals can be resolved. Hence, relation is even more fundamental to the notion of progress than is goal-directedness. Proper direction in one's life could not be had without proper relation of one individual to another.

Let us go to the history of philosophy to find various theories on the role of man and his relations to other men in society. At one end of the spectrum of available positions, we find Plato who claims in his *Republic* that the individual man falls into certain ranks. At the other end of the spectrum, Bertrand Russell holds to a theory of scientific progress in which the individual is largely reduced to a scientific object. Karl Marx, whose theory of progress culminates in a Utopian view, also plays down the notion of the individual. For him man is an ensemble of social relations. This description of man is consequent upon the fact that the individual is only an aspect of the Marxian dialectical process.

A detailed analysis of the above positions must be taken up for the purpose of detailing the limits within which one can envision the meaning of social relations necessary to progress. A philosophy that stresses a monadic view of the individual—a view of the individual as one that does not relate to others—is hard pressed when it comes time to analyze the meaning of progress, for social progress means social relation. If a philosophy stresses progress under the guise of process (as in Marx) or in relation to science (as in Russell), it does not allow enough room for a theory that the individual man enters into social relations.

Let us take a look at Plato's philosophy in detail. Plato's thought does not admit to the newness necessary for progressive action. His philosophical view ultimately falls back on the Greek notion that motion is cyclical. Newness means the cycle must be broken. Yet we find that the spirit of modern philosophies develops from a rethinking of Plato. A. N. Whitehead is so fond of the thought of Plato that he claims all philosophy is but a footnote to Plato. Moreover, when a philosopher demands that our judgments about the world demand some reference to a standard, we call him a Platonist.

As a philosopher-artist, Plato claims that the sensible world—the changeable world that we see around us—is an image of a model found in another world, the world of Forms or Ideas. Things we see about us in the sensible world are imperfect, but not totally or radically so, because they share in the perfect Form or Idea. In a relative sense, then, the sense world can be said to be perfect in that it shares in a Form. In many ways Plato's philosophy of image and model is very appealing. That there are models has been the topic of discussion of many thinkers even up-to the present day; however, the notion that sensible things are perfect through participation in Ideas has come under serious fire by many ancient as well as modern authors.

Now, for Plato, the being of things in the sense world is derived from Models. So, too, is their perfection. (Being and perfection converge in a very important way, for only Forms are being; only Forms are perfect in themselves.) But it is certainly more appropriate to say things in the world of Forms are being than to say sensibles are being. Forms are perfect, immutable Models; hence, the being of sensibles is in an important sense extrinsic to them.

Change is particularly relevant to the sense world. But such change can be seen as ordered only when looked at through the Ideas or Forms. In themselves the sensibles seem to have no rhyme or reason. In themselves they are much like a pure Heraclitean flux, which is historically considered as chaotic in view of the fact that the principle of contradiction is not operative in it. The models to the contrary cannot change. If they were to change, they could become "better" or "worse." This, however, is a characteristic only of imperfection. The Forms are always perfect—indeed, simplicities that do not even admit of possible or potential division. Insofar as they cannot change, they do not progress. Forms are what they are: completely perfect. In themselves sensibles cannot be called progressive either, for they are not normative. They get their normativeness not from themselves, but rather from the realm of the Ideas—which are also not progressive, as we said.

How does Plato know there are such things as Ideas? Not being able to find an example of perfect justice in the sense world, that world we observe outside of us, Plato takes another approach. He looks within himself where he claims to find an innate idea of justice, that justice according to which the sensible example or image is modeled. This knowledge from within is used in criticizing and analyzing the imperfect examples of reality found about us. The entire innate idea theory of knowledge is a kind of mysticism. It is the job of the philosophers to prepare themselves to get the proper intuitions. These intuitions of reality are much like those of an artist who intuitively conceives of a beautiful Mona Lisa which is used as a model for that which he will express on the canvas.

Is this intuitive (innate) knowledge progressive? No, not in any real sense of the word. The amount of knowledge that can be attained is limited to the number of perfect models or Ideas that exist—and there must be a finite number of Ideas; otherwise, knowledge would be finite or irrational. There can be no new knowledge. No one in this life has all the knowledge of the world of Forms, but he can recall only small parts of it in flashes of understandings (intuitions). In the words of Plato:

> Hardly after practicing detailed comparisons of
> names and definitions and visual and other sense
> perceptions, after scrutinizing them in benevolent
> disputation by the use of question and answer . . .
> at last in a flash understanding of each blazes
> up, and the mind, as it exerts all its power to the
> limit of human capacity, is flooded with light.[14]

Plato's theory of knowledge is intuitive, but his knowledge

is new only to the point that it is newly or freshly recalled.

Thus, for Plato (1) the Forms cannot be progressive; (2) the sensibles in themselves are not progressive; (3) there is only a finite amount of knowledge. That is true for all the Greeks. Consequently, novelty is not possible. Changes in knowledge are purely cyclical in nature. What we think is new now is only that which we knew at another time and forgot. It is only newly recalled.

Now, it is not every man in Plato's *Republic* that enjoys the privileged cognition—the intuitions—of the Ideas. This wisdom is available only to those of a certain rank. This rank concept is very strong in the *Republic,* for there is, for all practical purposes, no relationship among the ranks.

Persons in the *Republic* fall into three different ranks: the gold class, the silver class, and the bronze class. The gold class consists of the intellectuals. They order (command) the other persons, but do not give their subjects any reason for the commands given. Reason only pertains to the intellectual rank. They alone have the virtue of wisdom. The silver class consists of the warriors who guard the country. Plato refers to them as the watch dogs of the *Republic*. They possess the virtue of courage. The bronze class, the merchants, are endowed with temperance, for they need that virtue in order to carry out their task in society.

There is a relationship among individuals within the classes, but no relationship among the classes of persons. The lower class follows what the higher one commands, but does not necessarily know the reason it must. The noble lie enters the picture here. The persons in the higher class—the rulers—can tell the lower strata an untruth if it is for the preservation of order in society. The noble lie is certainly an example of the problem of irrationality cropping up in the social structure of Plato's *Republic*.

Going beyond Plato's philosophy for a while, let us dwell a bit more on the distinction between relationship and rank. Every relation must admit of ranks, orders, or classes of things or persons. But the notion of relation goes beyond that of rank. St. Thomas Aquinas brings out this distinction. He says:

> Order can be taken in two ways, either to signify degree only, so those who belong to one grade are said to be of one order, or to signify the relation which is between the various degrees, so the ordination is called order and in this way is taken concretely, so that an ordered degree is called an order.[15]

Aquinas refers to the use of the word "order" as degree or rank as a concrete usage of the word. This is in contrast to order as relationship, which is the abstract usage.

What Plato's social theory of the *Republic* lacks—and for that matter Plato's entire philosophy—is a philosophy of a relationship where relationship means unity-in-distinction, not distinction brought about by rank or degree.

The rank-concept and the relation-concept can be applied to our present-day society. In many respects the world of yesteryear trained individuals to fall into certain ranks or orders. There were all kinds of ranks—according to religion, job, social status, and the like. As we find ourselves approaching the twenty-first century, the "relation-concept" enters strongly on the social scene. In today's relation-conscious society we often hear terms such as "employee-employer relation" and "public relations."

Surely, the upshot of the new movement encourages individual progress (insofar as the person is aiming to perfect himself) and social progress (insofar as individuals relate to each other to perfect society). Let us put forth some examples of relation-consciousness. What does one mean by a good teacher? The answer, of course, is a teacher who relates well to his students. It is the relationship that allows the instructor to function well as an instructor. If the teacher does not relate (that is, if he cuts himself off from the students), the students' learning can be seriously hampered. Relationships involve the ability of the individual teacher to get the material across, to get the students to like the subject matter, and other such notions.

What does one mean by a good father of a family? Again, the answer lies in the father's ability to communicate or relate to the individual members of his family. A good father does not put himself in a certain rank (as father) due to his position and thereby refuse to reason with his family. He does not merely order the family to carry out his commands.

Political figures, religious leaders, and other prominent people in society today are beginning to realize that as good leaders they must get the persons under them to relate. With such relations the government or the Church as well as the family can continue to progress, but without such relationship progressiveness is hindered. In fact, the fewer relationships one has, the more difficult it is to carry out a job, for to cut oneself off from others means to lose a sense of the needs of others. If the class concept is pressed too far by leaders in society, persons tend to rebel. They want to revolt from their classes and become part of society at large. I am not advocating here that classes should or even will disappear. What I am advocating is that classes should not completely cut themselves off from each other.

In the discussion of social relations up to this point, special importance has been placed on the individual who enters into social relations. Social relations must aid the individual. Leonard Krieger in a *Review of Metaphysics* article also stresses the importance of the individual to a theory of progress:

> Progress requires creation, it requires too the conditions for creation, that is, it must be individual, free and concrete . . . only individuals and societies conceived as coincidences of individuals bear value; hence only such individuals are agents of progress, that is in an ultimate sense, for each individual is granted the right of his own absolute. Consequently, individuals are discontinuous in time; so is progress.[16]

The above text goes beyond the ancient Greek view in that it involves a discussion of the meaning of progress, but, nevertheless, the view of the individual man that it promotes is not far from that which Plato develops in his *Republic*. For Plato, it was said earlier, the individual falls into ranks, but there is no real relationship among the ranks themselves. Krieger talks about societies considered as coincidences of individuals. Such a view of society does not yield easily the notion of man as one who relates to other men; that is, as one who enters into social relations.

To stress creation and freedom is extremely important

in the consideration of progressiveness. If we do not allow the individual the freedom out of which creative activities spring, we do not have progressive activity. But to take the individual out of the relational context in which he exists—which in fact his very nature dictates—not only is a distortion of the meaning of the individual, but also leads to a distorted notion of progress.

Social relation, it was said earlier, can be considered as a criterion for social progress. Not to place importance on such relationship results in a conflict of aims and goals. Such conflict could mean the difference between world (or even domestic) peace and war. It could mean the use of atoms for peace or for destruction of mankind. Social relationship involves not only a "coincidence of individuals," but also a planned, rational, reasoned-out unity of aims. Maybe Krieger can opt for scientific progress, but if his notion of progressiveness is used solely as a criterion for progress in the hard sciences, it can lead to social chaos of the highest kind.

Krieger's notion of progress places far too much stress on the notion of man *qua* individual. Man, however, is not an atomic, unrelated unit. Even freedom of the individual—a condition for progress—must be considered in the context of man as one who enters into social relations. Otherwise, freedom means solely the absence of any restraint on the individual. Is man free to kill another man? No, his freedom does not allow him to do this. The fact that Krieger overstresses individual progress at the expense of social progress forces him to conclude that progress is, in the final analysis, an anachronism.

Krieger arrives at his conclusions as he attempts to get away from past theories that were tied in with evolution and teleology. Evolution implies a progression from a given state to a better one. Teleology involves a certain set of absolutes under which this progression takes place. These theories of the past looked up to a vague notion of a law of nature. Departure from this old philosophy means the introduction of novelty for Krieger.[17]

Raymond Aron in his book *Progress and Disillusion* also departs from the old-fashioned evolutionary theory, but his view of the individual man is quite different from that of Kreiger. He points out:

> Modern sociology no longer grants an immanent necessity to development of a global society and no longer dreams of utopia; it oscillates between heeding the microscopic (relations between individuals) and bending its efforts toward the totality, but without assuming the possibility of combining the two.[18]

Aron then goes on to explain, in a section of his book called "The Dialectic of Equality," the subordination of all to the decision of a few. He also realizes that persons do not only want to be equal but also want to be individuals.

The view of anthropologist Robert Briffault stands in opposition to the position stressed by Aron:

> The fatal fallacy that human improvement is the fulfillment of the individual was the faith of ages when only a few individuals could fulfill the potential of their lives; it no longer corresponds to social facts. It has in truth never corresponded to social facts, for the societies which have been built upon the sand of that fallacious faith have one and all encompassed their own destruction.[19]

Having considered philosophies that do give consideration to the individual in some sense—though not in a totally satisfactory way—let us proceed to examine the position of Bertrand Russell. His theory of progress plays down the individual man. Russell's view differs from all of the positions discussed. Let us immediately turn to his view on progress capsulated in *Mysticism and Logic*:

> To conceive of the universe as essentially progressive or essentially deteriorating is to give to our hopes and fears a cosmic importance which may, of course, be justified, but which we have as yet no reason to suppose justified. Until we have learned to think of it in ethically neutral terms, we have not arrived at a scientific attitude in philosophy.[20]

The text just quoted is representative of the scepticism brought about by Russell's inability to find natural reasons for occurrences of any type in the cosmos. But, causes are reasons, and, moreover, goals or ends are causes. Now, to claim that nature is progressive is to claim that it is goal-centered. Furthermore, goals are norms for action in an ethical sense. Russell's inability to discern them in nature—or his inability to find reason in nature—makes him claim the universe must be thought of solely in "ethically neutral" terms; that is, not in the light of normative action.

To be unable to assert reason in nature in any way has deeper implications. A universe that lacks reason also lacks relation. Therefore, Russell, in not being able to admit the reality of relations, is hard pressed when it comes time to advance a theory that would allow for the fact that man enters into social relations. The individual

man according to Russell is no more than the outcome
of accidental collections of atoms in a universe where
there are no ends or goals:

> That Man is the product of causes which has no
> prevision of the end they were achieving; that his
> origin, his growth, his hopes and fears, his loves
> and his beliefs, are but the outcome of accidental
> collocations of atoms; that no fire, no heroism, no
> intensity of thought and feeling, can preserve
> an individual life beyond the grave; that all the
> labors of the ages, all the devotion, all the
> inspiration, all the noonday brightness of human
> genius, are destined to extinction in the vast
> death of the solar system, and that the whole
> temple of Man's achievement must inevitably be
> buried beneath the debris of a universe in ruins—
> all these things, if not quite beyond dispute, are
> yet so nearly certain, that no philosophy which
> rejects them can hope to stand.[21]

In reality man turns out to be a "thing" in a world
where "things" are completely neutral;[22] that is, not know-
able as individuals. According to Russell, all that can be
known is the sensation or perspective from which we talk
about "things." From our perspective it is possible to develop a logical construct, an important part in Russell's
philosophy of science. But a logical construct lives only
in the constructing mind of the thinker.

Since Russell felt there was no evidence for reason
in nature, he publicly placed himself into the category
of atheists. Knowing Russell was an atheist, a woman once
asked him at a social gathering what he would say if, when
he died, he would discover in the afterlife that there ac-

tually is a God. Russell said, "Why, I should say, 'God, you gave us insufficient evidence. . . .' "[23] And evidence Russell insists he does not find, for he says norms cannot be grounded in nature, relations cannot be grounded in nature, and in fact we can never get to know things themselves in any way.

The obvious stress on science in Russell's philosophy presents difficulties in developing a theory of progress which accounts for the fact that man enters into social relations with others. But it would be unfair to Russell to say that his stress on science does not allow for a humanitarian outlook on reality:

> Nothing that goes against science has any chance
> of lasting success in the modern world. . . .
> Throughout the world science and industrialism
> must be accepted as irresistible and our hopes for
> mankind must all be within this framework. . . .
> It has at last become technically possible, through
> the progress of machinery and the consequent
> increased productivity of labor, to create a society
> in which every man and every woman has
> economic security and sufficient leisure.[24]

If science is successful, man profits, for science is what brings man security and sufficient leisure. The arts are helpful only in that they develop the imagination of man for the development of scientific hypotheses. This view of science and progress is found not only in his essays on education, but also in *Our Knowledge of the External World*.

Russell's universe is like a gigantic scientific experiment. The pacifism for which Russell is famous is an humanitarian move that complements his scientific view of the universe. If peace is had, the extinction of the world is prevented and, as a result, the experiment of man and the universe can continue.

Now let us place Russell's progress-theory up against the meaning of progress which this book promotes.

(1) In his own way Russell does come up with one possible solution to the problem of progress talked about earlier—that progress in one area such as science can cause regress in another area. There is for Russell only scientific progress. Everything is in some way reducible to science. So, there is no conflict with other areas.

(2) Russell's stress on science and lack of emphasis on social relations prevents him from grounding his humanism in nature. His humanism becomes a matter of constructualism or maybe even ends up an emotive theory —an alternative Russell himself might have to ponder a while.

(3) It may be granted that Russell has made a contribution to the field of science—especially in the writing of the *Principia Mathematica* with Whitehead. But it seems he stressed science far too much in his progress-theory. His view insists that science brings us comfort in living. This is true, but it also brings us woes.

(4) Russell does not have a progress-theory in any real sense of the word. He claims progress can be predicated of hypothesis-building, although the world is not progressive in any way. What Russell must confront is that he finds no reason to claim we are in the long run going anywhere with these hypotheses. So much for Russell.

Karl Marx also plays down the notion of the individual person in his philosophy, but for reasons other than Russell's. Taking the dialectical method of Hegel and applying it to history, Marx fashioned his philosophy of dialectical materialism in which all reality is a generation coming forth from a combination of opposites, a thesis and an antithesis. This combination of opposites forms a process that goes on and on. Now, it is not the individual in the process that is important; it is the process, a relation of individuals grouping into a kind of unity, that is important.

What kind of theory of human progress can such a philosophy as that of Karl Marx have? First, let us underscore that it is the process of development rather than the individual that is important for Marx. Man *qua* humanity in its developmental process and relation is important to Marx. The individual can be considered but must be singled out or in some way abstracted from the process. Hence, man becomes an ensemble of social relations:

> . . . [the] sum of productive forces, forms of capital, and social forms of intercourse, which every individual and generation finds in existence as something given, is the real basis of what the philosophers have conceived as the substance and essence of man, and what they have deified and attacked: a real basis which is not in the least disturbed in its effect and influence on the development of men.[25]

Marx further maintains:

> The social structure and the state are continually evolving out of the life process of definite individuals . . . as they really are, i.e., as they are effective, produce materially, and are active under definite material limits, presuppositions, and conditions independent of their will.[26]

If man then is not an individual, but the reality of man is considered in relation to some type of absolute and in some kind of transcendent sense in which all men are one and one is all, then human progress is more properly predicated of the overall process than of the individual persons in it.

Earlier it was stated that relationship is a condition for progress. Let us apply this notion to what has just been said with regard to the philosophy of Karl Marx. Certainly, relationship is a condition of progress for Marx, but proper qualifications and distinctions must be made.

It is important to notice that a balanced social progress lies between the two extremes (1) giving the individual all attention and society very little or none, and (2) giving society all and the individual very little or none. If it were not for the advancement of individuals, it would be impossible for society to progress. It is the minds of individuals that have advanced in science or economics or any other field. Important stress must be placed on the development of the individual. Terms such as the "mind of society" or the "public mind"—heard often nowadays (and not necessarily in connection with the philosophies of Marx or Hegel)—do not depict real entities. They might be considered as statistical averages; for example, the public mind on a certain point, when taken from a poll of some type, could be what 51 percent of the individuals in a certain area considered to be correct. It is not the "public mind" that thinks in the very strict sense of the word; it is rather the individual mind that contributes to the formation of the public mind.

Individuals in fact do not live alone. They cannot be explained as unrelated entities cut off from the overall picture. They need other individuals for their advancement in all areas. In fact the degree of success of individual advancement depends to a great extent on the way in which the person relates to other persons. Total cutting away of oneself from others can put one out of touch with advances that have taken centuries of work to bring about. Thus, more and better relations with others make for more and better advancement of both individual and society.

I am not advocating a static philosophy as opposed to an active, process philosophy. Instead, I claim that in the notion of relationship individuality, unity, difference, and distinction are all important to a progress-theory. Karl Marx puts important emphasis on certain of these characteristics. One element does not cancel out another and evolve into a greater degree and higher importance. For Marx, individuals must cancel each other out in a strange type of unity-in-relation.

One must not be naive about dissolving the social-individual tension established in society from time immemorial. No classless society in which everyone will be perfect will come about. The brunt of Marxian philosophy is to press for the achievement of this kind of Utopia. On the contrary, some kind of orders and ranks will always be with us, but we can strive for more and more relationship among the ranks. From such an openness will emerge the beginning of an understanding of one another. Such an understanding means social progress.

SUMMARY AND CONCLUSION

When John F. Kennedy became President of the United States, he predicted that many scientific firsts would come about in the 1960s as a result of the financial and scientific efforts being put forth around the time he took office. His prediction certainly came true. Before we reached the 1970s successful heart transplants were performed, man went to the moon and came back safely. Now in the mid-1970s there is even more promise for the future—maybe even interplanetary travel.

Despite the great scientific achievements, political and social unrest has risen to tremendous proportions. What if man cannot solve these problems? The answer: violence at home will continue. Despite the scientific advances, political and social problems loom high, not only at home but in the world at large. What if these cannot be settled? The answer: the possibility and maybe even actuality of catastrophe—more than just conventional war —nuclear war that could destroy the entire earth.

The thought of what the future could bring comes with great shock—the possibility that a settlement might be impossible. The world is disillusioned with what has come about on the social and political front. Yet we have to realize that all these problems have arisen despite advancements in science. In the twentieth century books have been written on progress in relation to all the topics just mentioned—violence, catastrophe, the future, and even disillusionment.

We have, then, two categories of events that have come about. On the one hand, the scientific advancements —and no one would deny them. And on the other hand, we witness the political and social chaos. In view of these two extremes, can we say we are progressing?

Scientific progress without social progress is of no avail to mankind. What good is the atom if it is used to destroy man? One of the greatest difficulties which we face today is that people in general extol the scientific experiment, but forget that *man* is the one that has brought about scientific achievements. It is *man* who got

to the moon. As some abstract entity called science is wor-
shiped, the importance of man gets lost. Man becomes no
more than a dot on the earth which in turn is a dot in
relation to all the planets in the universe.

Two tendencies can be singled out: the reduction of
man to a scientific object and the recognition of a scientific object as a discovery by man. Russell and many other
English philosophers tend to reduce man to a scientific
object. This tendency results in dehumanization. The
second trend asserts the importance of humanity above all
else. It is unfortunate that this trend does not mature.

A discussion of whether a reduction in scientific
progress would encourage social progress is purely academic. It is not a meaningful alternative, since we are
confronted with scientific progress. We must cope with
the complex problems that science has brought us. Scientific progress can be used to bring about good or bad
relations among men. The use of the atom for war rather
than peaceful purposes is constantly discussed. We are
faced with the problem of placing scientific progress under
the control of social progress to make them work together.

At present we have scientific progress. No one would
deny this. Numerous examples of advancements in medicine, physics, chemistry, and biology substantiate the claim
of scientific progress. In fact, some people claim we are
progressing on the scientific front more than we need to.
It is fairly common to hear persons nowadays state that
more than one or two moon expeditions are a waste of
time and money. But it is unlikely that such talk will im-
pede the natural curiosity of man to explore the unknown.

It is more difficult to say whether we are making
social progress or not. The world is changing more rapidly
than ever before. Sometimes we hear persons claim social

progress is made, while at other times a more pessimistic attitude prevails.

The purpose of this work is to probe the meaning of progress. We observed that progress means change for the better. But change must involve novelty or it just repeats itself. Furthermore, novelty becomes identifiable with revolution. But revolution spells out regress if taken to be an end rather than a means to an end.

Another facet of progress is end. Change must be directed to an end, otherwise it is not ordered change. End is a metaphysical as well as an ethical notion, for end means goal as normative. End must be considered in a relational context or a conflict of goals results. It is in fact out of this context of relationship that a discussion of social progress must arise. Individuals perfect themselves by relating to other people—they need others to fulfill themselves. Out of relationship springs creativity and freedom from which the individual develops. Insofar as relationship is central to any progress-theory, we can say that the more social relations prevail, the more social progress occurs. Relation, then, is a criterion for social progress.

Relationship means above all else communication. The fact that there is disagreement—even serious disagreement—does not mean advancement cannot prevail. In fact, differences, individual conflicting opinions, often pave the way for progressiveness, but the element of difference must not yield to chaos. Chaos results when communication is lost and the overall intelligibility is entirely fractured. If differences, on the other hand, are part of intelligible change, we need not fear regression.

The story of man's progress is not limited to one area, but progress appears in science, politics, social conditions, and other areas. Progress in one area can give rise to problems in another. When a significant advancement in one area translates into problems in many other areas, one is inclined to doubt the progress of the total culture. One has reason to entertain this doubt today, for scientific progress in our times can lead to social regress. The best way to cope with such a situation is to set down a condition under which we are certain social progress can be realized—namely, ideal relationship in which neither the individuality of the person nor the spirit of community is lost.

What is the value of analyzing the meaning of progress in our era? Certainly, it is not possible to determine the total meaning of progress for our century. This was not attempted in this work and in fact could not successfully be accomplished now. Only historians and philosophers in the distant future will be able to do this. Christopher Dawson, the author of *Progress and Religion,* claims that progress can fully be assessed only when the ideas of an age have begun to lose hold on the mind of the society and when the phase of civilization of which they were characteristic begins to pass away.[27]

We can set down some criteria for progressive social change and try to discern the role scientific advancement plays in social change. However, we can be sure that as as long as there is change, there is hope for change to the better.

Epilogue:
Man's Impatience
with Progress

Often the implicit image underlying statements about man's progress is the clear picture of a straight line of exactly spaced soldiers advancing across an open field into the brilliant setting sun of the future. A more accurate image would be the murky picture of a company of soldiers painfully infiltrating an enemy's heavily fortified jungle position. The advance is tortuous, dangerous, very uneven. One sector will yield quickly to the pressure of the infiltrating troops; another sector will counterattack with heavy fire power and drive the attacking troops back; in a third sector, the troops, confused by the unknown terrain, will double back on their tracks and perhaps fire on their own comrades. As a result, communication between groups is temporarily broken off; the overenthusiasm of some troops will impel them to advance so fast that their gains could be quickly wiped out by an enemy counterattack. The fearful caution and dithering of a second group will keep them far behind their comrades. It is not a case of each company advancing without thought of the other; they do inform, protect, hearten and tongue-lash each other. But if the advancing infiltrators do not regroup soon, all their specialized individual efforts may be partially wiped out. Their very advance is producing more and new problems.

If this second image of human progress is the more realistic of the two, then we are fairly warned that human progress involves many diverse factors, that these factors can support or hinder each other, that they advance at different rates (sometimes with dogged slowness, at other times with sudden spurts) and with varying strength of intersupport, and that unpredictable accidents can galvanize or paralyze progress.

Let us relate the conclusions of the Preface and three chapters to this image of the infiltrating companies of soldiers. First of all, each chapter tries to select out the basic factors which produce progress into the jungle of intricately interlaced future options—each infiltrating soldier is recognized and characterized. Next, an attempt is made to show how these basic factors are coordinated so that, like a carefully trained company of commandos, each factor, though autonomous, is shown to be hard put to exist and to operate without the teamwork of the other factors. Finally, the factors for progress and the network of their mutual influences are mapped out much as the senior officer tries to orient his company by pinning down each soldier's position and condition.

Because many factors must collude to produce progress, more than a few parameters must be used to measure progress. Further, because these factors are so mutually supportive or enervative, the measuring parameters must be applied to the societal flow of events simultaneously and correlatively. This complex operation of measurement will tax the patience of man. He will be strongly tempted to try shortcuts such as violent revolution. This is ultimately the crisis of man: his impatience with himself. Bernard Lonergan, the eminent philosopher of culture, puts this neatly: "The fourth, fifth and sixth volumes of Arnold Toynbee's *Study of History* illustrate abundantly and rather relevantly the failure of self-determination, the schism in the body social, and the schism in the soul that follow from an incapacity for sustained development."[1] Thus the previous chapters tried to indicate that the task of measuring the interlocking movements of human progress was not entirely hopeless. Indeed, the conviction underlying these chapters is that if man fails to make such an assessment and to plan accordingly, the world will eventually have good reason to be hopeless about itself.

PATIENTLY LEARNING TO SURVIVE PROGRESS

Chapter I explores five basic factors entering into the progress of civilization, no one of which can long survive without the other four: public morality, government structures, technological advance, scientific advance, and the need to plan for the future. Government structures offer the machinery for advancing civilization; however, they tend to run down unless the public morality of widely shared and strongly held common values is operative within them. But these two factors, in turn, cannot hope to help society or even to keep up with it unless their activities are carefully planned. W. T. Stace's capsulized definition of civilization as "organized goodness" is all too true. Within industrializing nations such planning, however, must be based on appropriate use of technology founded radically on new scientific advances. Thus all five factors for progress, because each is necessary to the existence of the other four, must be carefully coordinated.

For this reason, Chapter I insists that technological advance must be subordinated to scientific advance and that the two be used as means toward man's humanization. Otherwise technology and science can distract us from man's spiritual development. For there is a Janus-quality, a peculiar ambivalence, to technological and scientific advance. Though the latter can liberate man from manual drudgery, hominize the world with telecommunications, and multiply the options open to man's freedom, they can also substitute computer routines for man's freedom, accelerate change to the gradual disorientation of man, create an artificial environment of genetic engineering to which man is forced to adapt, and structure society into totalitarian procedures. The great fear of us all is that the present solutions to contemporary problems will breed future problems worse than the present set—unless the factors for progress are carefully integrated with humanistic values stressing man's unique dignity and destination.

In Chapter I, the problem of progress comes down to this: How does man coordinate the various ongoing solutions to our many cultural problems without employing some master plan which would stifle progress? We must have a single final goal by which we interrelate these developing programs-for-progress and by which we evaluate them. But can we be patient enough to let this final goal constantly develop as our struggle for solutions gradually clarifies and enriches this goal without ever making it totally accessible and comprehensible to us? Thus this final goal or supreme value becomes the basic criterion for progress and the source of subordinate values or criteria by which to assess man's technological and scientific progress. Concretely, this final goal would be the spiritual development of man. Man's crisis, then, is learning to survive the progress toward this goal as he struggles to keep the values of technology and science subordinate to this final goal.

PATIENTLY DEVELOPING OUR FRIGHTENINGLY COMPLEX CIVILIZATION

Chapter II selects out of the process of progress three basic factors: (1) *secularization,* the expansion of individual and collective personality through the specialized development and integration of knowledges and skills within and between their serving communities; (2) *secularity,* the various constellations of values derived from and directive of secularization; and (3) *secularism,* a particular secularity derived from philosophic scientism but claiming to be secularization itself and, therefore, asserting itself as the only viable value system. Chapter II takes note that specialization, if not periodically integrated, becomes trivial; and that secularization of the individual person makes secularization of his community possible, while individual secularization weakens if it is not supported by communal secularization. This cumulative development of individual and communal intelligence is progress itself since it enables man to penetrate ever more deeply into the world of persons, animals, and things and, through this marriage with the world, to become ever more human and ever more responsible for self, others, and civilization.

However, there is a qualification to be made here. Among the diverse secularities developed by man, some promote the secularization process better than others;

some even inhibit the process. For example, the secularity which tends to depreciate man's scientific knowledges because they are not directly theological and the secularity which implies that manual skills and work are below man's dignity both slow down the secularization process. Again, since that particular secularity called secularism depreciates any knowledge other than physical science and implies that no other secularity is truly viable within secularization, it so stunts the growth of man's personality as to enfeeble the secularization process at its very core. Thus an additional parameter for measuring progress would be the type of secularity which enjoys the widest currency at a particular point of secularization. Relevant questions to be asked regarding this secularity would be: Does it allow other secularities or value-systems to live? Does it include mystery and myth (the expression of mystery) so that secularization, which expands by the challenge of competing secularities and by feeding off myth and mystery, can advance?

Chapter II contends that once this philosophic understanding of secularization, secularity, and secularism is appreciated, then the manifestations of philosophic secularization on the economic, political, artistic, theological, technological, and other levels can be recognized. Further, these levels are seen to be promoted for evil or for good by various secularities (e.g., either to atomize or communalize man, either to stifle his freedom or to enhance it, either to center man's attention on the comfort of things or to focus his powers on the challenge of persons, either to trivialize man's artistic bent or to render it serious). Consequently, secularization, taken in itself or philosophically, is neutral and always good because it works for the humanization of man. But taken sociohistorically in its various manifestations (the economic, artistic, psychological, and so on), secularization can be either good or bad, since this latter quality depends on the healthiness of the secularity which predominates at the moment in the historical secularization process. As a result, regress is not only possible but observable in historical secularization.

The goodness or badness, then, of the secularization process can be measured by at least five parameters: (1) the depth of its specialization; (2) the width of its integration; (3) the growth of the individual person by means of this specialization and integration; (4) the growth of his community due to the same factors; and (5) the efficacy of the dominant secularity within individual and community to promote philosophic secularization. Of course, the secularization process is no longer a simple matter. Its complexity is often intimidating and sometimes overwhelming. So, man's present crisis is this: Can he remain patient with the complexity of life which he is busy building for himself?

PATIENTLY HARMONIZING SOCIAL REVOLUTION

Chapter III discerns three basic factors within the dynamism of progress: social harmony, the novelty of inventive intelligence emerging from free creativity, and scientific advance. Social harmony is common action toward a commonly accepted goal which is grounded in factual existence and not in a utopian mental projection. But in Chapter III social harmony does not mean social uniformity. For without the novelty of free creativity, progress would be frozen and life would become meaningless. Yet the novelty cannot be such that it removes the common goal and substitutes for it another goal; such radical change makes common action impossible and disrupts the continuity necessary to progress. This reveals that social harmony is the result of social relationships which somehow allow diversity in unity. The unity makes common action possible; the diversity assures that the common action is freely novelized, not necessarily routinized. Finally, what could scientific advance be without free creativity and how could social harmony be maintained in our scientific culture without scientific advance? Thus all three factors are interdependent in their promotion of progress.

This interdependence is seen graphically and its constitution of social relationships is delineated by contrasting the diverse insights of Bertrand Russell, Plato, Krieger, and Marx. Russell's scientism forces him not only to define progress as simply the developing hypotheses of physical science but also to envision man as a monad unrelated to the other monads constituting the universe. Consequently, Russell risks relegating progress to the confines of the human mind and allowing it to evaporate even from there. Plato's Ideas or Forms, the unchanging sources of all reality in the changing world, hardly lend themselves to real progress or dynamic relationships of novelty. More realistically, Krieger sees progress within the individual's development through creative activity; but he does not stress sufficiently that social relations contribute to the individual's growth. On the other hand, the absolutely reverse doctrine is taught by Marx, who sees man as simply the sum of social relationships and nothing more.

Across the spectrum of philosophic doctrine on progress, Bertrand Russell's bleak universe of unrelated atoms reveals the contrasting richness of relationships within our experience; Plato's frozen universe of static relations signals in contrast the warm world of dynamic relations within our lives; Krieger's insistence on individual development through free creativity calls attention to each man's dependence on others for his responsible growth; in turn, Marx's overemphasis of the deterministic society highlights the free individual within progress. Here it becomes clear that individual progress can happen only through social progress and vice versa, that the scientific advance extolled for its solitary splendor by Russell is really to be subordinated to social harmony, that social harmony is freely novel and yet carefully conserves what is necessary for common action.

The criteria of progress, then, become the number and the quality of those social relationships which allow both creative freedom and the consequent differences of meaning for the common goal and for the means of its pursuit. This is a social harmony so dynamic that it allows revolution which does not disrupt the common action. Yet it is at the same time so conservative that it will not allow any substitute for the common final goal. For these reasons, this is a social harmony whose progress demands patience and union between liberals and conservatives.

Converging Views on Progress

Rather astoundingly, from the diverse viewpoints of political science, social philosophy, and metaphysics of relation come converging conclusions about progress. First of all, the hope for man's future progress is seen to be based on his ability to coordinate the various solutions to diverse cultural problems so that they aid, rather than hinder and frustrate, each other. Chapter I attempts to coordinate the technological and scientific advances with the humanistic development of man's spiritual good. Chapter II tries to correlate individual and communal specialization and integration with the best secularity. Chapter III, in order to assure the richest social relationships, unites individual creative freedom with common activity toward a commonly accepted goal by subordinating scientific advance to this union. In all three instances, organized goodness is the aim; and the organization needed to achieve this goodness in man and community is amazingly complex as well as terribly demanding of intelligent patience.

Because of this complexity, every advance of civilization and culture is historically ambivalent in that it produces both good and evil. In addition, because man's freedom enables him to choose those values by which he hopes to achieve progress, each man's or each community's set of values can be more or less helpful for producing progress; that is, more or less productive of good or evil. For this reason, all three chapters stress the importance of planning the future and of choosing well the values that will guide this planning. Progress is not inevitable, nor is regress impossible. In all three chapters, there is a consensus that technology and science must be subordinated to man's spiritual development or humanization or dynamic social harmony.

Afterthoughts

The authors feel that, in response to Professor Roth's request in the Foreword, they have selected, interrelated, and evaluated rather precise criteria for defining and measuring progress. However, they do not think for a moment that they have responded to his second request for judgments on how human fulfillment presently is the criterion for progress; this would demand that they apply their criteria empirically to the present situation and to the present plans for man's future. This is the further task for social scientists—in collaboration with philosophers, theologians, trade unionists, mothers and fathers, businessmen and women, artists, farmers, and so on.

Professor Roth asked a third penetrating question: Are the authors working in a purely secular framework or does a transcendent source or goal underlie their understandings? Actually all three chapters touched on this point—but without elaborating, lest a second book begin to take shape. Underlying each chapter is the conviction that a transcendent source or goal of progress is operative in societal life. When Chapter I speaks out against any final solution to the problem of progress, its concern is that a powerful group of zealots will impose upon mankind a master blueprint for progress and thus turn modern civilization into a somewhat genial and smothering concentration camp run by cultural commissars. Far from excluding a single final goal or supreme value toward which man gradually approaches by a diversity of strategies and paths, Chapter I calls for a public morality, common normative action toward an ultimate common goal or value. Here Chapter I suggests that a transcendent goal is necessary for man's spiritual development through the means of scientific progress. Chapter I sees government action or the imposition of some official ideology upon the people as futile for achieving progress; historically, any absolute finality created solely by man's decrees has proved, in its rigidity, narrowness, and naïveté, quite wasteful of progress. Yet there is a finality operative in man's history. Otherwise progress would be pure illusion and chaos would now reign. Man implicitly forms his ideals according to this finality or supreme value. In this way, Chapter I sees man's history as open to the constant influence of a transcendent source and goal for human progress; that is, for human growth of spirit.

Though the approach of Chapter I to the transcendent is more positive than the approach of Chapter II, the latter focuses a strong light upon society's supreme, world-englobing value, namely, its world-view or *Weltanschauung*. This world-view poses sharply the problem: Which is the supreme value of life—the world alone without God or God present in the world? The solution to this problem provides two radically different secularities for animating the secularization process. The first option is taken by the godless secularity called secularism which, by excluding all mystery from the world and by shrinking man's consciousness to the single knowledge of physical science, drastically enfeebles secularization. The second option of theistic secularity leaves man open to a variety of knowledges and to the richness of mystery which is wider and deeper than all man's knowledges and skills. It offers an immanent yet transcendent being worthy of man's total dedication to the progress of secularization.

Finally, Chapter III hints at a transcendent source of progress through a logical unfolding of what progress is. It takes the following steps along a path toward the transcendent:

(1) Without progress, life is simply an absurd wandering in circles of chaos.

(2) Without a goal, progress ("the better") becomes indefinable, unobservable.

(3) Without a normative ethics for achieving this goal, progress cannot happen since there is no path to the goal.

(4) Without a *common goal* for the normative

ethics, people cannot cooperate so that progress becomes possible for both community and individual.

(5) Without an *existent* (i.e., objective) common goal (one that is not pluralized into diverging goals by unreal subjective relativism), the common action becomes ever less effective.

(6) Without such a goal allowing for *creative novelty* in its pursuit, society becomes homogenized by deadening routines; in fact, individual freedom risks being lost utterly.

(7) Yet without this same goal demanding that the *individual's spontaneity* be *subordinated* to the needs of communal cooperation, the common pursuit of this goal is at least jeopardized.

Steps 6 and 7 point quietly to the need for a transcendent mediator who, to make social progress possible, must discreetly and simultaneously protect individual freedom from the oppression of society and the common good of society from the pillaging of the individual.

Clearly, all three chapters are united in the conviction that progress itself, as seen historically and as analyzed philosophically, is actually the ever fuller development of the human spirit. These chapters carry the grave doubt that man's spirit grows well when his development is unrelated to a supreme spirit whose immanent presence, while within the collective spirit of man, is yet much more than the latter could ever be. For progress to be possible, much more to be existent, there must be operative within it a single, transcendent, ever-novel source and goal. This Transcendent Being seems to be slowly unfolding the richness of his presence in the world's evolving history and to be beckoning the world on to greater progress, to fuller revelation of himself.

Yet the crisis of man badly blurs this insight into

the transcendent. Man is impatient at the complexity of the civilization he has himself built, at his own smallness in the face of the huge problems generated by the very successes of science and technology, at the slow pace of some changes for the better, at this civilization's ambiguous ability to promote good and evil simultaneously—sometimes within the same event. Man needs to take confidence from past progress: he is driving out ignorance with vast educational systems; he heals and cures by means of the most intricate medical technology; he has invented the agricultural technology to feed the whole world sufficiently; he has made strangers neighbors through telecommunications; he has developed social security systems to provide for emergencies of ill health, old age, widowhood; his growing knowledge of the world through physical science and of himself through the life sciences as well as through theology and philosophy can make his life richer than ever before; he has forged new instruments of peace, such as the United Nations and its satellite agencies, and worldwide ecumenism and the contributing churches.

Clearly, without the possibility of progress, man is absurd. Without adequate progress, man is hopelessly mocked and frustrated by his own powers of freedom, inventiveness, and love. Yet progress is not inevitable; it must be planned patiently with the best scientific instrumentation and with the clearest philosophic and theological visions of value. Progress must be suffered as much as enjoyed. Will man be patient enough under the suffering? That is the critical question. For, in desperation, he could attempt to solve his problems by a sweeping and violent revolution which might destroy many societal structures painfully erected over the many years, and make the solution of the new, revolution-induced problems terribly difficult, if not impossible. Evidently, confidence in his past progress is proving not enough to keep man patient. Is it possible that he also needs a transcendent source of confidence to escape the ultimate impatience of self-destructive revolution?

Notes

CHAPTER I

1. See John B. Bury, *The Idea of Progress: An Inquiry into Its Origin and Growth* (New York: Macmillan, 1932).

2. W. R. Inge, *The Idea of Progress* (Oxford: Clarendon Press, 1920).

3. Robert Bierstedt, *The Social Order* (New York: McGraw-Hill, 1957), p. 556.

4. Julius Gould and William L. Kolb, editors, *A Dictionary of the Social Sciences* (New York: The Free Press of Glencoe, 1964), p. 545.

5. Carl L. Becker, *Encyclopedia of the Social Sciences* (New York: Macmillan, 1951), Volume 12, p. 495.

6. René Dubos, *A God Within* (New York: Charles Scribner's Sons, 1972), p. 230.

7. Lewis Mumford, *The Myth of the Machine: The Pentagon of Power* (New York: Harcourt Brace Jovanovich, 1970), p. 261.

8. Robert Bruce Lindsay, *The Role of Science in Civilization* (New York and Evanston: Harper and Row, 1963), pp. 198–99.

9. Gerard Piel, *The Acceleration of History* (New York: Knopf, 1972), pp. 125–26.

10. Matthew Melko, *The Nature of Civilizations* (Boston: Porter Sargent, 1969), p. 73.

11. Lewis Mumford, *Newsweek,* July 7, 1969, p. 61.

12. Jacques Ellul, *The Technological Society* (New York: Knopf, 1964).

13. William Kuhns, *Environmental Man* (New York and Evanston: Harper and Row, 1969).

14. Erich Fromm, *The Revolution of Hope* (New York and Evanston: Harper and Row, 1968), pp. 32–33.

15. *New York Times,* January 10, 1970, p. 10.

16. Robert L. Sinsheimer, *New York Times,* September 1, 1968, p. 18.

17. Theodosius Dobzhansky, *Genetic Diversity and Human Equality* (New York: Basic Books, 1973), p. 31.

18. H. J. Muller, "What Genetic Course Will Man Steer?," *Bulletin of the Atomic Scientists* 24 (March, 1968), p. 8.

19. Viktor E. Frankl, *Man's Search for Meaning* (New York: Washington Square Press, 1967), p. 209.

20. David E. Apter, *The Politics of Modernization* (Chicago: University of Chicago Press, 1965), pp. 10–11.

21. Robert L. Heilbroner, *The Prospect for Man* (New York: W. W. Norton, 1974).

22. Herman Kahn and B. Bruce-Briggs, *Things to Come* (New York: Macmillan, 1972), pp. 210–11.

23. John McHale, *The Future of the Future* (New York: George Braziller, 1969).

24. Dennis Gabor, *The Mature Society* (New York and Washington: Praeger, 1972), pp. 44–45.

25. Daniel Callahan, "The Sanctity of Life," in Donald R. Cutler, editor, *The Religious Situation* (Boston: Beacon Press, 1969), p. 297.

26. Peter Drucker, *The Age of Discontinuity* (New York and Evanston: Harper and Row, 1969), pp. 27–28.

27. Pierre Teilhard de Chardin, *The Future of Man* (New York and Evanston: Harper and Row, 1964), pp. 229–30.

28. Victor Ferkiss, *The Future of Technological Civilization* (New York: George Braziller, 1975).

29. Alfred North Whitehead, quoted by Lawrence K. Frank in "The Need for a New Political Theory," *Daedalus*, Summer 1967, p. 816.

30. Everett Mendelsohn, Judith P. Swazey, and Irene Taviss, editors, *Human Aspects of Biomedical Innovation* (Cambridge, Mass.: Harvard University Press, 1971), pp. 19–20.

31. René Dubos, *A God Within*, p. 256.

32. Max Kaplan and Phillip Bosserman, *Technology, Human Values, and Leisure* (Nashville and New York: Abingdon Press, 1971).

33. Fred Best, editor, *The Future of Work* (Englewood Cliffs, N.J.: Prentice-Hall, 1972).

34. René Dubos, *A God Within*, p. 261.

35. Ian G. Barbour, editor, *Earth Might Be Fair* (Englewood Cliffs, N.J.: Prentice-Hall, 1972).

36. Lynton Keith Caldwell, *Environment: A Challenge to Modern Society* (Garden City, N.Y.: The Natural History Press, 1970).

37. Daniel P. Moynihan, "Politics as the Art of the Impossible," *American Scholar*, Autumn 1969, pp. 580–81.

38. Robert J. Steamer, "The Far Side of Freedom," *Polity*, Winter 1969, p. 212.

39. Albert H. Teich, editor, *Technology and Man's Future* (New York: St. Martin's Press, 1972).

40. Daniel Callahan, *The Tyranny of Survival* (New York: Macmillan, 1973), p. 58.

41. Quoted in John Wilkinson, editor, *Technology and Human Values* (Santa Barbara: Center for the Study of Democratic Institutions, 1966), p. 20.

CHAPTER II

1. Albert L. Schlitzer, C.S.C., editor, *The Spirit and Power of Christian Secularity* (Notre Dame, Ind.: University of Notre Dame Press, 1969), p. 194.

2. Larry Shiner, *The Secularization of History* (Nashville: Abingdon, 1966), p. 26. See also p. 35.

3. Ibid., p. 35.

4. Jacques Maritain, *The Range of Reason* (New York: Scribner's, 1952), pp. 193–94.

5. Robert Nisbet, *The Social Bond* (New York: Knopf, 1970), pp. 370, 388.

6. Edward Schillebeeckx, *God, the Future of Man* (New York: Sheed and Ward, 1968), pp. 67–68.

7. For a concise definition of myth see Henri Frankfort et al, *Before Philosophy* (Baltimore: Penguin Books, 1967), p. 16. The book is a brilliant exposition of the mythopoeic as contrasted with the speculative.

8. A. C. Crombie, *Medieval and Early Modern Science* (Garden City: Doubleday Anchor, 1959), Vol. 1, pp. 5–6 and passim. These two volumes amply illustrate how rudimentary scientific thought is developed by practical concerns.

9. For a study of organization as the manifestation of secularization, see Dietrich von Oppen, *The Age of the Person* (Philadelphia: Fortress Press, 1969), pp. 42–73.

10. Plato's *Republic* is an amazingly clear presentation of many major elements in the secularization process: distinction of knowledges and skills, divisions of labor, balance of powers, the principle of organization (applied

to government, armed forces, and even entertainment), the social as magnified expression of the individual. But upward mobility between classes is not stressed. For elaboration of this, see D. J. Hassel, S.J., 'Eπitndɛυµα or Civic Vocation in Plato's *Republic*," *Modern Schoolman* 41 (1964), Part I, pp. 145–57; 41 (1964), Part II, pp. 251–62.

11. I have listed brief descriptions of some of the many levels of secularization in "Secularization, Secularity, and Secularism," *Working Papers on Problems in American Life*, Vol. I of the General Survey of the Society of Jesus, North American Assistancy, edited by Bruce F. Biever, S.J., and Thomas M. Gannon, S.J. (Chicago: Argus Press, 1969), pp. 58–59. To anyone familiar with Bernard Lonergan, S.J., and his philosophic work, especially his *Insight* (New York: Philosophical Library, 1957), it will be clear how indebted I am to him for his theory of how knowledges are historically differentiated and integrated in a constant dialectic of growth and decay. Jacques Maritain's *Three Degrees of Knowledge* (New York: Scribner's, 1959) has also been formative.

12. Roland Robertson in "Sociologists and Secularization" (*Sociology*, Sept. 1971, Vol. 5, No. 3, pp. 297–312) relates how value judgments affect not only the defining of secularization by sociologists but also their testing of its presence (or absence) and its effects.

13. Obviously, the following description of secularity is deeply influenced by *Social Construction of Reality* (Garden City, N.Y.: Doubleday Anchor, 1967), by Peter L. Berger and Thomas Luckmann.

14. Hans Urs von Balthasar in *Science, Religion, and Christianity* (Westminister, Md.: Newman, 1958), shows historically, psychologically, and theologically how,

within the secularization process, a man's *Weltanschauung* determines his own self-evaluation and his relationship with God. In fact, Balthasar uses man's developing self-concept as the measure of progress in world history.

15. A collective effort to explore and evaluate the relationship of secularization and prayer has been edited by Christian Duquoc, O.P., in the Concilium Series: *Secularization and Spirituality* (New York: Paulist Press, 1969, Vol. 49). It offers more than a glimpse at the way in which secularity works within secularization.

16. The reciprocal causation between secularity and secularization can be appreciated only in its historical unfolding. Under this aspect, Roger Aubert has edited a helpful volume of historical essays in the Concilium Series: *Sacralization and Secularization* (New York: Paulist Press, 1969, Vol. 47). The individual articles trace secularization from the early Church up to the present in Western Christianity; one essay is devoted to this phenomenon in the Eastern Church. A remarkable condensed historical essay on the secular and the sacred is Albert Mirgeler's *Mutations of Western Christianity* (London: Burn Oates, 1964), especially pp. 130–50.

17. If one wished to check how diverse and rich are secularities within simply one area, e.g., Christian secularity, he could consult H. Richard Niebuhr's classic *Christ and Culture* (New York: Harper and Row Torchbooks, 1956).

18. On this point, confer T. F. McMahon's rich article "Secularism," in the *New Catholic Encyclopedia* (New York: McGraw-Hill, 1967, Vol. 13, pp. 36–38) where he states that of itself secularism is neither theistic nor atheistic even though the American secular humanism of this century looks to be antitheistic.

19. As an example of zealous secularism I would cite Corliss Lamont's *The Philosophy of Humanism* (New York: Philosophical Library, 1957), especially p. x where his zeal is evident and pp. 9–12 where he states the basic tenets of his secularism. A second example would be Hans Reichenbach's *The Rise of Scientific Philosophy* (Berkeley: University of California Press, 1963), particularly pp. 295–96, 300–302.

20. The books of Mircea Eliade are particularly graphic in their exploration of religious symbolism and myth, especially his summary *The Sacred and the Profane* (New York: Harper and Row Torchbooks, 1961).

21. A singularly compact and sensitive historical report of the perils involved in relating science to religion through philosophy of science and philosophy of religion is given us by Ian G. Barbour in *Issues in Science and Religion* (Englewood Cliffs, N.J.: Prentice-Hall, 1966).

22. Dietrich von Oppen, op. cit., pp. 136–41.

23. See Charles Davis, *God's Grace in History* (New York: Sheed and Ward, 1967), pp. 41–42.

24. Peter Berger makes much of the ultimate plausibility structure in his *The Sacred Canopy* (Garden City, N.Y.: Doubleday Anchor, 1969).

25. N. J. Demerath III and Phillip E. Hammond, in *Religion in Social Context* (New York: Random House, 1969), sketch the relationships between sectarianism (differentiation) and secularization where the latter is taken as a watering down of religion, a contamination of the sacred by the ordinary (pp. 104–5).

26. Piet Smulders, S.J., has noted how this problem (the crippling of socialization by hyperspecialization) preoccupied Teilhard de Chardin. See his "Teilhard and the Future of Faith" (*Christian Witness in the Secular City*,

edited by Everett J. Morgan, S.J., Chicago: Loyola University Press, 1970, p. 11).

CHAPTER III

1. Herbert Spencer, *Social Statics or the Conditions Essential to Human Happiness Specified and the First of Them Developed* (New York: D. Appleton & Co., 1866), p. 80.

2. W. R. Inge, *The Idea of Progress* (Oxford: Clarendon Press, 1920), p. 34.

3. John Morley, "Some Thoughts on Progress," *Educational Review* 29 (1905), p. 7.

4. *Business Week,* August 29, 1970.

5. *New Yorker,* June 6, 1970, pp. 92 ff.

6. G. K. Chesterton, *Heretics* (London: John Lane, 1905), p. 36.

7. A. J. Todd, *Theories of Social Progress* (New York: Macmillan, 1918), p. 94.

8. Leonard Krieger, "The Idea of Progress," *Review of Metaphysics* 4 (1951), p. 483.

9. Stanley Casson, *Progress and Catastrophe* (New York: Harper & Bros., 1937), p. 3.

10. Hannah Arendt, *On Revolution* (New York: Viking Press, 1963), p. 35.

11. Ibid., p. 41.

12. Crane Brinton, *The Anatomy of Revolution* (New York: Vintage Books, 1965), pp. 24 ff.

13. Ibid., pp. 250 ff.

14. Plato, *Seventh Letter* 344b, translated by L. A. Post, in *Plato: Collected Dialogues,* ed. E. Hamilton and H. Cairns (New York: Pantheon Books, 1961), p. 1591.

15. Thomas Aquinas, In II *Sent.,* 9, 1, 1, ad 2.

16. Krieger, pp. 486–87.

17. Ibid.

18. Raymond Aron, *Progress and Disillusion* (New York: New American Library, 1968), p. xv.

19. Robert Briffault, "Is Man Improving?" *Reasons for Anger* (New York: Simon & Schuster, 1936), p. 264.

20. Bertrand Russell, *Mysticism and Logic and Other Essays* (London: Longmans, Green & Co., 1925), p. 44.

21. Ibid., pp. 47–8.

22. Bertrand Russell, *Our Knowledge of the External World* (London: Allen and Unwin, 1917), p. 73.

23. *New Yorker,* February 21, 1970, p. 29.

24. Bertrand Russell, *The Selected Papers of Bertrand Russell* (New York: Modern Library, 1927), pp. xiv–xv.

25. Karl Marx and F. Engels, *German Ideology* in *Marx and Engels,* ed. Lewis S. Feuer (New York: Doubleday, 1959), p. 258.

26. Ibid., p. 246.

27. Christopher Dawson, *Progress and Religion* (New York: Sheed & Ward, 1933), p. 4.

EPILOGUE

1. Bernard J. F. Lonergan, *Insight* (New York: Philosophical Library, 1957), p. 632.

Index

137

About the Authors

FRANK J. YARTZ, Ph.D., is an associate professor of philosophy at Loyola University of Chicago. At Loyola he teaches undergraduate and graduate courses in the history of philosophy, particularly in the areas of Plato, Aristotle, and Thomas Aquinas. He has published articles on ethics and Ancient Greek philosophy. His works appear in *Medieval Studies, Southwestern Journal of Philosophy,* and *Modern Schoolman.*

DAVID J. HASSEL, S.J., Ph.D., is an associate professor of philosophy at Loyola University of Chicago where he teaches courses in the Philosophy of Evolution, Metaphysics of Culture, Being and God, Philosophy of Man, Philosophy of Religion, Secularization Theory, and the Philosophy of St. Augustine. He has published a chapter in *Working Papers on Problems in American Life,* book reviews in the *Modern Schoolman* and *Theological Studies,* an article in *Proceedings of the Jesuit Philosophical Association.* He is presently completing two books.

ALLAN L. LARSON, Ph.D., is a professor of political science at Loyola University of Chicago, teaching both undergraduate and graduate courses in comparative political systems. His articles and essays on political and social science subjects have appeared in *Educational Forum, Social Studies, Social Education,* the *Midwest Quarterly,* and the *Delphian Quarterly.* He is currently writing a book on comparative political analysis.